How to Discover

Your Personal Life Mission

Finding Your Passion
and Living Your Dream

by

John Morgan, Ph.D.

and

Steve Johnson, M.A.

PRESS

How to Discover Your Personal Life Mission
Finding Your Passion and Living Your Dream
by John Morgan, Ph.D. and Steve Johnson, M.A.

Printed in the United States of America

ISBN 978-1-60266-474-6

www.xulonpress.com

Contents

Section IV   How to Write Your PLM Statement and How to Align Your Life

Chapter One

Introducing Personal Life Mission:
Your Place in This World

"It takes a lifetime for a man to know who he is, like who he is, and be who he is."
Charles Swindoll

"Pettiness is the result of a life with no high purposes."
George Will

"Nothing contributes so much to tranquilizing the mind as a steady purpose
— a point on which the soul may fix its intellectual eye."
Mary Wollstonecraft Shelley

In Addition to Being Pathetic, She Was Mean

"I'm not ready to go!" she screamed. "I'm not worthy. I'm not ready to go!" She

screamed it over and over again, all night long in her nursing home bed.

I knew Mrs. K's family and had visited her on several occasions. She was dying of

uterine cancer, and the end was getting closer. Her screams could be written off as

mindless hysteria, but her family felt she was having genuine regrets for a wasted life.

She was nice enough to me, but her life story was one of selfish absorption. She

married a young man and then cemented herself to him like a barnacle cements its head

to a pier. That was her only monumental decision in life. She literally lived his life. In her

early days, she went with her husband to his construction job and sat in the car all day

waiting for him. She left her children at home to get themselves ready for school and then

to take care of themselves after school while she sat in the car.

Her husband hadn't helped the situation. He doted on her as if she were an invalid. "He did everything for her," her family said. When he died, so did she for all intents and purposes. She was nothing more than an appendage.

On top of being pathetic, she was mean. She was cold and uncaring to her children, grandchildren, and great-grandchildren. In her last days, her family was struggling to make peace with her. They felt she had betrayed them by living such a useless, egocentric existence. She lived with no sense of purpose outside of herself.

That is wrong. It is wrong whether it is Mrs. K or a multi-millionaire who lives with essentially the same life values. And the regrets at the end can be more painful than the physical pains of cancer.

On the other hand, a life lived on purpose not only gives the deepest kind of satisfaction and joy, but it will also pass on benefit to others. That is the kind of life most of us really want to live. Most of us want to fulfill a personal life mission that helps others and leaves the world in better shape. That is what the Personal Life Mission system is about.

Just As I Am

"The only true happiness comes from squandering ourselves for a purpose."
                                                                        William Cowper

The Reverend Billy Graham's autobiography, *Just As I Am*, is on my list of top ten favorite books. I was inspired by the life of Dr. Graham. He has traveled the globe more, met more influential people worldwide, and has been friends with more American presidents than any other person I can think of. What a life! But the most striking feature of his life is the fact that he gained a sense of purpose, and of calling, of vocation. It became the guiding light of his life.

You can bet that when the end of his life comes, the outpouring of affection from around the world will be phenomenal. What a contrast between a life lived on purpose and one just lived! It is to this end that we, John and Steve, live our lives on purpose and with passion, and that we present to you this Personal Life Mission system. It is a simple tool to help you come to terms with the most profound thing in life: your very purpose. May you discover the purpose that will impassion you and inspire others.

What Is a Personal Life Mission?

"Many persons have a wrong idea of what constitutes true happiness. It is not attained through self-gratification but through fidelity to a worthy purpose." Helen Keller

Definition: Your Personal Life Mission is the body of work for which you have been chosen and for which you are being designed so that you will do some good things for some people. It is your life's purpose — your worthy purpose, as Helen Keller stated. As the PLM logo depicts, it is your place in this world.

Your PLM prepares you to take your place in this world. The key word there is "prepares." Do you believe in luck? Well, luck is when preparation meets opportunity. Mike Shanahan, coach of the Denver Broncos football team, talks about preparation in his book *Think Like a Champion*. "The difference between someone who is successful and someone who isn't is not about talent. It's about preparation. So much of what successful people do ... is tied to the powerful principle of preparation. It enables people to move ahead, stay ahead, and live ahead.... The way to bring out the best in you is not by chance, but rather through preparation."

When God placed his call on my life, I didn't immediately go out and start pastoring a church. No, I went into church preparation, which is called seminary. I didn't know if I was going to be able to get a job when I got out; but I did know that if I didn't prepare, I would never get a job. Preparation leads to success.

The Personal Life Mission system is based on some of the most powerful ideas from three separate, but in many ways, overlapping disciplines: theology, psychology, and management theory. In other words, it's based on who made us, how we were made, and how we can do what we were made to do. Let's look at each discipline and how it fits into the PLM system.

PLM Ideas From Theology: Who Made Us
Divine Purpose and Design

There is divine purpose to history, life, and your life in particular. There is divine design in history, life, and your life. You don't know if you believe that? Let's look at the evidence in the Bible that there is divine purpose and design to these three areas.

The Bible presents a linear world view. It presents human history as a process that had a beginning and that is moving toward a conclusion. The events between the beginning and the conclusion define the destinies of individuals in time and for eternity. What we do in this life matters on a grand scale. Our actions in time have consequences for eternity. We live in a system of divine purpose.

The Bible also presents God as being the director of the flow of history. He is moving world history forward on the course that he intends in the timing that he sets.

The biographies of men and women in the Bible show how there is divine purpose and design even at the level of our individual lives. Consider the story of Joseph in Genesis 37-50. Joseph was the favorite son of his father, causing much jealousy in his brothers. In order to get back at the bragging Joseph, the brothers eventually sold him to some Midianites who eventually sold him to the Egyptian Potipher's household. There, Joseph was falsely accused of attempting to rape Potipher's wife and was thrown into prison, where he gained a small amount of renown as an interpreter of dreams. Many years later, the Pharaoh needed a dream interpreted and one of the former prisoners remembered that Joseph, who was still rotting in prison, interpreted dreams. Joseph was released and interpreted the Pharaoh's dream that a famine of seven years was coming. This gave them enough time to prepare. Pharaoh put Joseph in charge of the financial well being of Egypt, and Egypt alone was able to eat through the famine.

But the story doesn't end there. Remember Joseph's brothers? Eventually, they come to Egypt hoping to find food, and through some bizarre manipulations realize that Joseph is their brother. They, of course, worried that Joseph might seek revenge against them. But listen to Joseph's words. "Do not be distressed and do not be angry with yourselves for selling me here, because it was to save lives that God sent me ahead of you....God sent me ahead of you to preserve for you a remnant on earth and to save your lives by a great deliverance. So then, it was not you who sent me here, but God" (Genesis 45:5, 7-8).

God's design and purpose at the level of individual lives is clearly seen. Further, the biographies of Noah, Abraham, Moses, Joshua, Deborah, Esther, David, Peter, Paul, and many others show divine purpose and design. We see that God puts the right people in the right places at the right times to do the right things in his will. As Mordecai says to his niece Esther, "Who knows but that you have come ... for such a time as this?" (Esther 4:14)

We also see an amazing fact; God begins to prepare people for their roles in his purpose in history even before they come to faith in him. In fact, he even begins before they are born.

> For you have created my inmost being; you knit me together in my mother's womb. I praise you because I am fearfully and wonderfully made; your works are wonderful, I know that full well. My frame was not hidden from you when I was made in the secret place. When I was woven together in the depths of the earth, your eyes saw my unformed body. All the days ordained for me were written before one of them came to be .
>
> Psalm 139:13-16

The New Testament teaching on spiritual gifts is another evidence for the divine purpose and design for our lives. In Romans 12, 1 Corinthians 12, and Ephesians 4, we are taught that God has given Christians special divine abilities to fulfill his work. "But life is worth nothing unless I use it for doing the work assigned me by the Lord Jesus..." (Paul in Acts 20:24 in *The Living Bible*) and "It has always been my ambition to preach the Gospel where Christ was not known..." (Paul in Romans 15:20).

One of the most profound statements in the Bible about salvation and what God has done for people in salvation is found in Ephesians 2. It shows a dramatic contrast in the condition in which people exist prior to salvation and after salvation. It also shows

God's intention not only to save people from judgment but also to save them to their divine purpose in life. Paul, the writer of Ephesians, could write some complicated sentences and paragraphs. But consider his core ideas in Ephesians 2:1-10, as we boil it down to the following core phrases:

"You were dead in your sins...

But God made us alive in Christ...

And seated us in the heavenly realms in Christ...

To show His grace...

For it is by grace you have been saved...

For we are God's workmanship created in Christ Jesus to do good works which God prepared in advance for us to do."

From biblical theology we see a clear statement that there is both purpose and design to our lives.

The Witness of Natural Law

God has placed this truth about his purpose and design into the hearts of people, even those who would not consider themselves Christians or even particularly religious. Consider the popular art of Disney's animated movies. The common theme that runs through *The Little Mermaid, The Lion King, Hercules*, and *Mulan* is the life-struggle to grasp and fulfill a significant purpose. Millions of dollars are spent by consumers like us for these and similar movies that tug at the deepest parts of our humanity and affirm our inner thirst for purpose and divine destiny. The intuitive craving for and belief in a higher purpose comes from the fact that God has created us for high purposes.

Joy

There is one other piece of theological truth that fits in the PLM concept. Remember Mrs. K from the beginning of this chapter? She epitomizes this theological truth. Self-centeredness produces misery, but doing what we can uniquely do to benefit others produces joy. True fulfillment comes from serving others. This doesn't require a Ph.D. degree in theology to figure out. It is common sense. It is the center of most religious beliefs. It is certainly core to Christianity because the Bible presents God as the embodiment of the world's most important force: love. When we live to bless others, we imitate God. As we progress through the PLM system, you will see more and more that your PLM is not about you as much as it is about how God designed you and is going to use you to bless others. When God called Abraham, he gave him a mission. God said, "I will make you into a great nation and I will bless you; I will make your name great, and you will be a blessing" (Genesis 12:2). Abraham, like all of creation, was blessed to be a blessing.

So, whether we look at biblical theology or a natural witness to truth, we see powerful evidence that there is a purpose and a design to our lives. We have a Personal Life Mission.

PLM Ideas from Psychology

What? Psychology? Isn't that secular? There are some Christians today who are very frightened of psychology. But there is no reason to be. There was a saying I first learned in seminary that has echoed down from Augustine and Aquinas: All truth is God's truth. What that means is that there are some truths that aren't found in the Bible but are true nonetheless; and if they are true, then they come from God who is Truth. For example, there aren't a lot of mathematical truths in the Bible, and yet we don't dispute the fact that angles of a triangle add up to 180 degrees. That's true. That is the way God created the world.

The same can be said of psychology. There are just some ways that the world and the people in it act because of the way God made them. Psychology has been misused at times, but that doesn't negate the truth that it contains. The truth that it contains comes from God, the source of all truth. What truth does psychology contain, and how does it relate to Personal Life Mission?

Motivation. Our behavior comes from inner motivations. That is a very simple but important foundation from psychology. We are seeing that motivations come from our personality, our experiences, and our desires that are in our hearts. The PLM system seeks to unlock some of those motivations because they are part of our personal design.

Abraham Maslow (1958) explained motivation as the fulfillment of a hierarchy of needs. Lower needs such as physical safety, food, and shelter come first. If these are met, people are motivated to higher needs like being accepted by others. Maslow called the highest level of motivation "Self Actualization." This level of motivation moves people to be things and do things that fulfill their highest sense of calling and purpose.

Psychometry. Psychometry is the measurement of personality or psychological traits. Over a thousand psychometric tools are developed and published each year. In the PLM system, we use the psychometric assessment tools that have been developed by Steve

Johnson of the Strategic People Development. The assessments in chapters 2-3 come from Steve's psychometric tool called the Chemistry Match™. The assessments in chapters 6-8 come from Steve's psychometric tool called the PathMaker™. Both of these assessments have been used effectively for many years with Steve's clients and affiliates. You will read the stories of some of those people in this book. These psychometric tools help reveal the design of our personalities. We believe our personalities have been designed to fit our purpose.

PLM Ideas From Management Theory

Management theory as an academic discipline is not very old. The Father of Modern Management, Peter Drucker, just passed away in 2005. Management theory is concerned with effectiveness. It seeks to answer how individuals and organizations can be effective.

As we study management theory we believe one of the core concepts that has grown from it can be said this way:

Put your most

On your best

For your greatest.

To be effective at achieving our greatest accomplishments in this life, we must discover what we do best and place most of our resources on it (Drucker, 1979). We must place most of our time, energy, money, resources, and creativity on what we do best in order to achieve our greatest. For organizations, this kind of thinking is called strategic advantage (Hatch, 1997). The Personal Life Mission system will lead you to discover your best so you can put your most on it.

There is a prevalent error going around that needs to be straightened out just a little. The error is the idea that you can be whatever you want to be. What? You mean I can't? The truth should read, you can be whatever you want to be, but you can't be all you want to be. Have you ever met someone who had to be the best at everything? Annoying, aren't they? And when they run up against someone, as they inevitably will, whom they can't best, their lives are ruined. We can't do everything with excellence. We must choose. And, man, is that liberating! We don't have to do everything. God created us to do certain things with excellence. What can I do with excellence? What is my best? Your PLM will define your answers.

Fifteen Reasons Why You Should Discover Your Personal Life Mission

1.   **Love.** As you do what you do best for others, you will be showing love. Those who give love are loved.

2.   **Joy.** There is an inner joy in giving your best to worthy purpose.

3.   **Peace.** Inner harmony comes from following your heart of hearts.

4.   **Success.** As Zig Zigler says, "To get what you want out of life, help others get what they want out of life."

5.   **Effectiveness.** If you aim at nothing, you will hit it.

6.   **Motivation.** Our personal sense of what we are striving for energizes us for the work it takes to accomplish it.

7.   **Achievement.** Pro-active people accomplish more things and greater things.

8.   **Self-Image.** Knowing your Personal Life Mission will give you a balanced self-image. You will be able to admit your weaknesses without fear and affirm your strengths without pride.

9.   **Priorities.** Knowing your PLM will establish what is important and what's not. It will give you the tool to say "yes" and "no."

10. **Time Management.** You can better manage the ultimate non-renewable resource: your time.

11. **Education.** Your PLM will give direction for educational goals, as you become a life-long learner with purpose.

12. **Career.** Your PLM will direct your career management through a process of becoming more and more on-target with each move.

13. **Money.** Not only will you probably make more of it as your work becomes more effective, but you will also have a life principle that will guide the management of money.

14. **Marriage.** You will discover that marriage is a mutual partnership that brings two PLMs together. That doesn't sound too romantic, but believe us; it can lead to lasting romance.

15. **Parenting.** Your PLM will guide your parenting goals, and it will give you a desire to prepare your children to discover their PLMs.

A Personal Life Mission is the ultimate life-management tool. It is the guiding principle for everything. It is not just a career thing. It is the umbrella that covers everything.

These fifteen reasons have all been demonstrated in the lives of people who have discovered their PLMs. There is another reason you should discover your PLM. To see it, you have to discover the big picture of what your life will be.

The Seven Stages of Adult Life

As we consider the research of Gail Sheehy (1995), E.H. Erikson (Miller, 1993), and Elliot Jacques (Jacques & Cason, 1994) on adult development and life cycles and add our own observations, we propose there are seven stages of adult life.

15-25: The Age of World Discovery. This is the time when you are experiencing the world for yourself and forming your basic views of life. Spiritual formations happen here. Key relationships are established, including marriage and children. Key ideas are shaped from education, people, books, and travel.

25-35: The Age of Work Discovery. This is the time when assumptions about work and personal abilities are tested. There is often a searching among several careers to find one that fits.

35-45: The Age of Self Discovery. After twenty or more years of work, we face mid-life transition and begin reevaluating what we have learned from our world discovery and work discovery. We start asking more existential questions: Who am I? What is my purpose? Why do I do what I do? Am I fulfilled? Is this all there is to life? Is this what I want to do with the rest of my life? This age is often a fork in the road to recycled frustration or personal growth and purpose.

45-55: The Age of Effectiveness. Applying the knowledge of who one is and what one does best can lead to a great time of effectiveness. At this age, physical and mental strength is high. Energy matched with working on-target produces effectiveness.

55-65: The Age of Efficiency. This is an age when one is wise enough to focus energy efficiently to get the most done with the least effort. This is the ultimate time of working smarter, not harder.

65-75: The Age of Influence. Having lived long enough and well enough, one can influence others. This is the time when wisdom can guide others and others readily recognize it. The power of personal presence can motivate others to get their lives on track.

75-and up: The Age of Power. One is seen as the icon or embodiment of an idea, movement or cause. This person can get away with almost anything. An example of this is what Mother Theresa did at the National Prayer Breakfast in Washington, D.C. with President Bill Clinton several years ago. She got up to speak and blasted him for his support for abortion. You can say those things when you're 75 and you've been living your life on purpose. By this age, there is a polar separation in how people are viewed: either as people of purpose and power or as people of meaninglessness and irrelevance. The difference is determined by whether or not they got their lives channeled in the right direction earlier.

The reason you should discover your Personal Life Mission is so you can pass through the stages of life with increased meaning and growing effectiveness. In the end, you do not want to look back with regret; you want to be looked upon and looked to with respect. As Kenneth Hildebrand said, "Strong lives are motivated by dynamic purposes."

How to Discover Your Personal Life Mission

The Personal Life Mission Worksheets are in Appendix A-C and are the tools we provide for you to build your personal notes as you go through this book and the PLM process. Visit TheJohnMorganCompany.com to order the PLM Worksheet.

The goal is to fill in the Personal Life Mission statement in Appendix C. This is the general statement of life purpose. It has three sections. The first section is your one sentence PLM statement. This one sentence says what it is that you do and for whom you do it. "My Personal Life Mission," wrote Georgia, "is to help women see their value in God's eyes and rise to achievement in that confidence." This PLM statement came from the details in the boxes on the left side of her PLM worksheet. Georgia's desire is to help women who are lacking confidence in their personal worth to gain a new view of themselves and act on it. And she is doing just that.

The second section is a list of the four main ways in which you will try to fulfill your PLM. Georgia's four "how to's" were:

1.   To model a healthy self-esteem and achievement.

2.   To develop a speaking business to women.

3.   To have a ministry in my church to women.

4.   To develop a consulting business for women.

The third section is a list of dreams or goals that are general. They do not necessarily have to tie directly to the PLM statement, although over time they almost always do. Here are some of Georgia's general dreams and goals:

1. To be spiritually mature and to grow throughout my life.

2. To have a great marriage that supports my husband's PLM.

3. To raise my children to fulfill their PLMs.

4. To be physically fit as a lifestyle.

5. To be a life-long learner and to earn a Ph.D. degree.

6. To cultivate some deep friendships.

7. To travel broadly in a speaking business.

8. To earn $50,000 a year through my speaking and consulting.

9. To travel to Europe.

10. To help 10,000 women rise from insecurity to achievement.

As you can see, Georgia has high dreams. Some will scoff at her dreams (and by the way, we do not suggest you share your dreams with just anyone), but over time her Personal Life Mission will guide her to fulfill part of what is in her heart of hearts. She will fulfill what she is designed to do. And who knows? She may even exceed fulfilling every one of her dreams by the end of her life. Can you imagine how rewarding that would be?

The Nine Pieces of Your Personal Design

Refer to the Personal Life Mission Worksheet in Appendix A. This nine-box square is where the PLM process begins. We will walk you through filling out your unique personal design in these nine areas. Most people have not identified their design in one of them. You will discover all nine, and the picture you see may change your life.

We will begin with the center column of boxes. We call these your "Present Wiring." These boxes are where you will fill in the results of three very powerful personality assessments. Don't be afraid. They are not tests! There are no wrong answers possible. They simply identify your best personality characteristics.

In chapter 2 we will lead you through the Personality Temperament assessment. You will discover why you approach life the way you do.

In chapter 3 we will lead you through the People Power assessment. You will discover how you best relate to others.

In chapter 4 we will lead you through the Project Zone assessment. You will discover what part of a project is the zone where you naturally excel. It will also help you see where you best fit in an organization and what kind of organization best suits you.

The information from these three boxes alone has changed many peoples' lives for the better in their families and careers.

Next we will go to the three boxes on the left. These boxes are where you will list key life-shaping items from your personal history. These will be powerful ideas in shaping what you want to do with your life. The first box is where you will list your best defining experiences. We will lead you through that in chapter 5. The second box is where you will list your worst defining experiences. Don't panic; this is often a very private matter and you may keep it that way. We will lead you through this box in chapter 6. Then we will lead you through an assessment of your abilities and some exercises that will help you identify what you do best. This will be in chapter 7.

Finally, we will go to the three boxes on the right. In these boxes you will list the key forces that are shaping your destiny. In chapter 8 we will help you identify the main areas of interest in your head. In chapter 9 we will help you discover your Essential Outcomes in your heart, or what you must get back from your work to keep wanting to do it. And finally in chapter 10 we will help you understand the passion in your gut. This is the final and often most important piece of all.

Your Summary Bridge

The middle PLM worksheet in Appendix B is the summary bridge. It involves looking at the overall picture of your nine PLM pieces and looking for the main theme or story. You will identify what you do better than anything else and for whom you want to do this. In chapter 11, we will lead you through this bridge. Filling out the bridge prepares you to begin writing the first draft of your Personal Life Mission statement.

Writing the First Draft of Your PLM

The first draft of your PLM is very important. It will not be perfect, but it will be the first step to a new way of life. It will help you think in ways that will change what you do for the better. We will give you pointers and examples of how to do this in chapter 11.

This PLM system is a toolbox. This toolbox is to get your life on target and to keep it there. To keep it there, you need to get out the tools and review your PLM pieces every six to twelve months and edit your PLM statement to fit your new experiences. Your basic PLM direction will probably not change over your lifetime, but your understanding of what you should be doing will become sharper and sharper every time you review and revise it. I (John) have been doing this since I was 25. Today, I'm over 40, and I still have the same basic PLM, but I understand what I should be doing with my time and energies 100% more clearly than I did back then. I look forward to my next stage of life, 45-55, when I will really be effective!

Living Your Dream: The Formula for Success

In chapter 12 we will give you the formula for success in living your dream. Chapters 1-11 are all about helping you identify your dream. Chapter 12 is a no-nonsense wisdom and a research-based guide to fulfilling your PLM. There are four factors for success that we will share with you. If you will define your PLM well and apply the formula for success, you can get there.

God's Pleasure

Most of us have heard of Eric Liddell, the sprinter in the 1924 Olympics whose story was told in the film *Chariots of Fire*. Eric was a Scottish missionary to China. His sister, Jennie, wanted him to return to China, but Eric wanted to try for the Olympics first. His words to Jennie were, "I believe that God made me for a purpose, but he also made me fast. And when I run, I feel his pleasure. To give it up would be to hold him in contempt ... to win is to honor him." When his heat for the Olympics came up on a Sunday, however, Eric declined to run because it would go against God's law. He was firm on this point and a teammate offered to let Eric run in his heat on Thursday. A committee member, after the decision, noted about Eric, "The lad is a true man of principle. His speed is a mere extension of his life."

"When I run, I feel his pleasure." Yes, most of us have heard of Eric Liddell. But do we realize that we are all Eric Liddell?

What is it in your life that gives God pleasure? When do you feel his smile warm upon your face as you fulfill the purpose he has given you? You might know, as Eric did, exactly what that purpose is. In that case, the PLM can help you sharpen that vision, clarify it until it is sharp. Maybe you don't know what it is, but you know that you want your life to count, to be significant. The PLM will help you unearth the treasure that God has created you to be.

To all those who want to achieve their best in this life, to all those who want to finish life with no regrets and deep satisfaction, to all those who want to fulfill their destiny, we challenge you to discover your Personal Life Mission.

Chapter Two

Discovering Your Personality Temperament:
The Stew That Is You

John's family makes a Mexican stew that is wonderful. The ingredients simmer together giving off an aroma that smells divine. And when it's eaten in a tortilla — ecstasy!

When we talk about your personality temperament, we are talking about the combination of personality ingredients that make your personality unique. It is your flavor — the flavor that's been simmering your entire life. It is the stew that is you.

Some Background on Personality Temperament

The word "temperament" dates back to before the 15th century. It originally meant the proportioned mixture of elements. It later came to mean a combination of opposite qualities like hot and cold or moist and dry which make up a substance.

The earliest record of the word "temperament" used to describe personality dates back to 1471 (Barnhart, 1988). It was observed that people's temperaments seemed to be more-or-less characterized by four types:

Sanguine (which comes from the word for blood) people were those who were full of life and cheerful.

Choleric (which comes from the word for bile) people were those who were short-tempered.

Phlegmatic (which comes from the word phlegm) people were those who were mechanical and cold-natured, like they had a cold.

Melancholic (which is like our word melancholy,) people were those who were depressed.

The temperament assessment we use was developed by Steve Johnson of Strategic People Development. It is the temperament section of the Chemistry Match™ and it is based on four "constructs" or categories of opposite personality traits from the theories of Carl Jung (1971). This assessment is about twenty years old. It has been improved over the years and has been affirmed by thousands of clients who have used it and found it both accurate and helpful in making decisions based on it.

The Four Personality Temperament Traits

The four personality temperament traits evaluate how you experience your environment, process that experience, then act back on your environment. The process looks like this:

Your Environment	Four Opposite Characteristics
How you take it in:	Internal . . . . .Social
How you react to it:	Realist . . . . Futurist
How you decide on it:	Thinker . . . . .Feeler
How you act on it:	Planner . . . . Adapter

Discovering Your Personality Temperament

The next pages contain Chemistry Match questions and statements to identify your personality temperament. For each statement or question check the one response that best represents how you perceive yourself to be most of the time. Don't sweat the contrasts too much. If you're having difficulty with one, look beyond the mere words to the principle involved. For instance, a woman who took the test stressed a little over the question about the telephone (#8). She said she hated the telephone, but because it was the only one she answered in the A column, she feared she had done something wrong, or that she wasn't reading the question right. Steve told her that it was what was behind the question: how did she feel about being interrupted? When she changed "telephone" to "e-mail," her answer changed. She loves e-mail, loves meeting new people through e-mail and doesn't mind the interruptions from it one bit. She's a social creature down the line. Remember, there are no right or wrong answers, and these answers represent how you perceive yourself most of the time.

Set 1   **Internal . . . . Social**

1. I mostly prefer to work ...ᴬ

   A. Alone, in a place where I can concentrate.

   B. Around people, where I can exchange ideas.

2. I most often .ᴬ

   A. Ponder what I am going to say before speaking.

   B. Decide what I am going to say even as I am speaking.

3. I generally have my ideas worked out ... *B*

      A. When I can write them out or line them up in my mind.

      B. When I can express them to others verbally.

4. I prefer to leave social settings like church or parties . *A*

      A. Before most and without a lot of fanfare.

      B. After I have finished talking with everyone I want to.

5. A special birthday party for me would be . *A*

      A. A great dinner with my spouse or a close friend or two.

      B. A surprise party with a lot of friends and fun.

6. My best work is usually a result of my *B*.

      A. Pondering problems and coming up with solutions.

      B. Interacting with others to solve problems.

7. I become emotionally drained from . *A*

      A. Too much contact with people.

      B. Too much isolation from people.

8. I mostly view the telephone as *B*

      A. A valuable tool for work but a big interrupter of my time.

      B. A valuable tool and a great way to stay in touch with others.

9. I need ... *A*

      A. Quiet places to go and be alone for planning and reflection.

      B. Social interaction so I can bounce my ideas off others.

10. I am ...ᵇ

    A. Often vulnerable and easily hurt by criticism.

    B. Usually confident and in control.

As _6_   **Bs** _4_   **Totals for Set 1**

Set 2   **Realist . . . . Futurist**

1. I generally read ...ᴬ

    A. Sequentially, cover to cover, looking for details.

    B. Sometimes randomly and always looking for the big picture.

2. I'm generally ᴬ...

    A. An inspector, evaluator, nuts-and-bolts type of person.

    B. An inventor, designer, creative-ideas type of person.

3. I usually prefer to be ᴮ...

    A. Conventional and practical.

    B. Original and innovative.

4. I prefer to work in a job that is ...ᴮ

    A. Solid, is part of a good system, and has good job security.

    B. Inspiring because I am working for a great cause.

5. I would rather be around .ᴮ

    A. People with common sense and ordered lives.

    B. People with vision and exciting lives.

6. I see myself as B.

      A. Realistic and down-to-earth.

      B. Creative and shooting for the stars.

7. I would rather B

      A. Do a job right, even if it takes more time.

      B. Get the present job done with and move on.

8. I prefer to work with B.

      A. Facts, known data, and historically proven methods.

      B. Concepts, innovations, and explorations.

9. When I hear a new idea for a product B

      A. My mind looks for the proof it can work.

      B. My mind pictures the new product working.

10. My normal work rhythm seems to be B.

      A. To pace myself and keep plodding to get the job done.

      B. To work in cycles of intense effort.

      As _2_ **Bs** _8_   **Totals for Set 2**

Set 3   **Thinker . . . . Feeler**

1. I generally make decisions A.

      A. On principle, fact, and logic.

      B. By my personal values and how it will affect people.

2. I have a tendency to *A*

    A. Hurt other people's feelings unintentionally.

    B. Seek to please people.

3. What I value most is *A*

    A. What is right.

    B. What works for people.

4. My motto would probably be *B*

    A. "Let your head rule your heart."

    B. "Go with your heart."

5. I believe that *A*

    A. Principles or facts are more important than circumstances.

    B. Circumstances are just as important as principles or facts.

6. I want others to *A*

    A. Treat me fairly and justly.

    B. Affirm me as someone who has value.

7. When people need to be reprimanded *B*

    A. I can do it because I know it is the right thing.

    B. I struggle with it because I don't want to hurt them.

8. I'm considered to be (like Star Trek characters) *B*

    A. Impersonal and logical (like Spock or Data).

    B. Personal and feeling (Like Counselor Troi).

9. I get into trouble because ..^A.

      A. People falsely assume I don't like them.

      B. I get too involved in helping others with their problems.

10. If I were a teacher, I would concentrate on ..^B.

      A. Teaching my students the content they need to know.

      B. Relating to my students to see what they mostly need.

As <u>6</u> Bs <u>4</u>   Totals for Set 3

Set 4   **Planner .Adapter**

1. I generally would rather ..^A.

      A. Plan my work and work my plan.

      B. Go with the flow or "play it by ear."

2. I generally like ..^A.

      A. A well thought-out plan.

      B. Spontaneity.

3. I normally ..^A.

      A. Like to get things "wrapped up" and decided quickly.

      B. Take time to explore all the possibilities and options.

4. I like to ..^A.

      A. Make a list of what I need to do and prioritize them.

      B. Just plunge in and tackle a project.

5. I like to act .B.

   A. Without wasting too much time in decision-making.

   B. After taking my time in making a good decision.

6. My projects seem to look like ..A.

   A. I am taking them one at a time.

   B. I have too many "irons in the fire."

7. Life is to be .B.

   A Regulated, planned, and controlled.

   B. Pondered, understood, and valued.

8. I do tasks A.

   A. Sequentially and in order of priority.

   B. Randomly and in spurts.

9. I make decisions A.

   A. In a quick and clear-cut way.

   B. With some hesitation and doubts.

10. My idea of a vacation is ..B.

    A. To have an organized and planned time of enjoyment.

    B. To hang loose and just do whatever happens.

As 6 **Bs** 4   **Totals for Set 4**

Total your answers from each of the four sets and transfer them below.

Set 1: How I Take in My Environment: My "Sensor"

A: Internal   B: Social

  (Total) __6__   (Total) __4__

You tend to analyze and ponder life   You tend to experience life as an

in a vivid world in your mind.   interactive event with others.

Set 2: How I React to My Environment: My "Processor"

A: Realist   B: Futurist

  (Total) __2__   (Total) __8__

You react to new things with caution,   You tend to react with vision and a

looking for proof, facts, and reasons.   mental image of how things could be.

Set 3: How I Decide About My Environment: My "Decider"

A: Thinker   B: Feeler

  (Total) __6__   (Total) __4__

You tend to decide by logic, reason,   You tend to decide things personally,

and without too much emotion.   Trying to be fair and helpful to others.

Set 4: How I Act on My Environment: My "Actor"

A: Planner   B: Adapter

  (Total) __6__   (Total) __4__

You tend to be orderly, organized,   You tend to be spontaneous, flexible,

and you like to follow the plan.   and dislike too much structure.

Now transfer your totals to your Personality Temperament box on your PLM Worksheet (Appendix A). Do this by writing the word for your dominant characteristic and the number of your score for that characteristic. You can think of the numbers as percentages.

For example:

1. Internal   90%

2. Futurist   80%

3. Thinker   90%

4. Planner   70%

In a minute you will also write the name of your temperament combination and some key themes that strike you as important in the same square on your PLM worksheet.

The Four Opposite Temperament Characteristics

1. Are You an "Innie" or an "Outie": Internal or Social?

No, we are not talking about your belly button! We are talking about how you like to take in the world.

Internal

If you prefer to internalize, you tend to focus more on your own inner world of the mind. You feel energized by what goes on in your head. You tend to be more interested and comfortable when your work requires most of your activity to take place inside your head. The work you do in your head may be presented to others for their benefit or use, and you may enjoy presenting it, displaying it or explaining it. But your best productivity comes from taking time to reflect on what you are fixing or creating.

Here are some typical characteristics of internal people:

* Like quiet for concentration

* Have trouble remembering names and faces

* Work on a project of high internal interest and lose track of time

* Are interested in the ideas and theories behind a job or experience

* Dislike telephone interruptions

* Think before speaking and use an economy of words

* May prefer to communicate in writing

Social

If you prefer social interaction, you tend to focus on the outer world of people and the external environment. When you are with people, you are energized by what is going on in the world around you. You tend to direct your energy toward people. You probably would rather get a point across by speaking instead of writing. You tend to think out loud. You tend to like action and to experience life.

Here are some typical characteristics of social people:

* Like variety and action

* Are good at greeting people

* Are impatient with long, slow jobs

* Lose track of time when enjoying good conversation

* Are interested in how others do their jobs

*	Enjoy talking on the phone

*	Like to be around others in the work place

*	Sometimes act or speak without thinking it through

*	Like to work out problems by brainstorming with others

2. Do You Look to the Past for Proof or to the Future for Inspiration:

Realist or Futurist

How do you react to new ideas? Do you look to the past for proof and evidence that it can work, or does your mind envision it working?

Realist

If you are a realist, you use all your senses to evaluate situations and ideas to see if they are practical. You accept the limitations that are part of everything in life, and you work within the rules. You are down-to-earth and steady. You have a good memory and can work with a large number of facts.

Here are some typical characteristics of realists:

*	Are aware of the uniqueness of each event

*	Focus on what works

*	Like to have established ways of doing things

*	Enjoy applying what has already been learned

*	Work steadily with a realistic idea of how long it will take

*	Usually reach a conclusion step by step

*	Seek to avoid unnecessary risks

*   "If it ain't broke, don't fix it"

*   Are careful about facts, precision, and sequence

Futurist

As a futurist, you see the world through your intuition and mental images of what can be. Your internal compass guides you toward meanings, relationships, and possibilities that go beyond the limitations of past experiences. You look at the big picture and look for the patterns. You like to see new possibilities and new ways of doing things. You value imagination and inspiration.

Here are some of the typical characteristics of futurists:

*   Are aware of new challenges and possibilities

*   Focus on how to improve things

*   Dislike repetitive work

*   Enjoy learning new things

*   Work in bursts of energy fueled by enthusiasm

*   Follow inspiration and gut instincts

*   May be wrong on facts or leap to conclusions

*   Will sacrifice precision for progress

*   Can over-complicate simple ideas or tasks

*   Search for why things are as they are

*   "If it ain't broke, break it"

In the movie *Twilight of the Golds*, David Gold is a man with a vision to make an opera of Wagner's *Ring Cycle*. This is a huge undertaking, fraught with many problems, one of which is the Cycle is 15 hours in length. This brings up the question of feeding people during the show. David, after listening for a few short moments to various arguments, bursts out, "Why must we waste our passion on food?" He is a true futurist. Don't bother him with the practicalities!

3. Do You Make Decisions Based on the Facts or the Effects: Thinker or Feeler?

If you look to the facts and logic to make your decisions, you are a thinker. If you look to the effects a decision will have on others you are a feeler. Think of the past television series, The *X-Fil*es. Scully was a thinker. She looked to logic, science, and facts to explain the strange phenomena that she encountered. Mulder, on the other hand, was a feeler. He made his decisions based on his own intuitions or what "felt" right to him.

Thinker

As a thinker, your primary way of processing information is through your thinking. Your thinking predicts the logical consequences of any particular choice or action. You decide objectively on the basis of logic and cause and effect. You analyze the evidence even when the conclusion can be unpleasant. You seek an objective standard of truth and will naturally analyze the details to see what is wrong with things.

Here are some of the typical characteristics of thinkers:

*   Put things in logical order

*   Respond more to people's ideas than their feelings

*   Predict logical outcomes

* Want to be treated fairly

* May hurt people's feelings unknowingly

* Good at analyzing problems

* Prefer to work with things and ideas rather than people

* Find emotional expression sometimes uncomfortable

* Would prefer to read a news magazine

Feeler

As a feeler, your primary ways of making sense of the world and arriving at conclusions is through your ability to sense how actions affect others. You do not require logic as much as you do solutions to human problems that work. When making a decision for yourself, you tend to ask how much you care or how much personal investment you have for each of the alternatives. You may like to deal with people and are likely to be sympathetic, appreciative, and tactful.

Here are some common characteristics of feelers:

* Enjoy harmony and work toward it

* Respond to people's values as much as their ideas

* See the affects of choices on people

* Need to be affirmed and praised

* Sympathize with others

* Dislike telling people things that are unpleasant

* Enjoy pleasing people

* Take an interest in the person behind the job or idea

*   Would prefer to read about people

4. Do You Get Things Done by Cruising or Sailing: Planner or Adapter?

There are basically two kinds of boats: cruisers and sailboats. Cruisers rely on their engines. Sailboats rely on the wind and currents. Planners are like cruisers; they set their course and go. Adapters are like sailors; they set sail and respond to the conditions, constantly making adjustments along the way.

Planner

If you take a planning attitude, you tend to live in a planned, orderly way, wanting to regulate life and control it. When you use your planning function, you like to make decisions, come to closure, and get on with it. You prefer to be structured and organized and you want things to be settled.

Here are some common characteristics of planners:

*   Plan their work and work their plan

*   Like to get things done and over

*   May decide things too quickly

*   May dislike interrupting the project they are on

*   Find satisfaction in reaching a conclusion

*   Want only the essentials needed to begin their work

*   Use lists as agendas for action

*   View punctuality as a moral issue

*   Tend to do things in their order of priority

*   Dislike having someone change the plan

Adapter

If you are an adapter, you tend to live in a flexible and spontaneous way. You gather information and keep your options open. You seek to understand life rather than control it. You like to stay open to experience. You enjoy and trust your ability to respond to the moment and to whatever comes along.

Here are some common characteristics of adapters:

  *   Do not mind leaving things open to last-minute changes

  *   Adapt well to changing situations

  *   May hesitate in making decisions

  *   Want more information to decide

  *   Can have too many "irons in the fire"

  *   May have trouble finishing projects

  *   Accomplish a lot under pressure

  *   Use lists as reminders of all that has yet to be done

  *   View punctuality as a preference

  *   Tend to do things in order of convenience or preference

  *   Dislike the boredom of routine

There is a wonderful scene in the movie *Parenthood* that depicts the differences between Planners and Adapters. Steve Martin has just quit his job and his wife informs him that she's pregnant with their fourth child. After a heated argument, the grandmother wanders in and tells them about riding the roller coaster at the fair. Some people don't like the roller coaster, she points out. They would rather ride the merry-go-round or the

Ferris wheel that don't really go anywhere. They're safe — risk free. But the roller coaster! On the roller coaster, you have twists and turns and you feel that your stomach is dropping out. It's unpredictable. Steve Martin, the planner, imagines himself on the roller coaster, clinging to the bar, not enjoying the ride because things aren't going as planned. His wife, on the other hand, just sits back and enjoys the ride. She's an adapter.

What Stew Recipe Are You?

As with John's family stew, you now know the ingredients that go into the wonderful stew that is you. What flavor do your ingredients simmer into? There are sixteen combinations, each with their own unique flavor.

1. Social-Futurist-Feeler-Planner: "The Mentor." Desires to lead others. Enjoys building people in their abilities. Sees potential in others.

2. Internal-Futurist-Feeler-Planner: "The Prophet." A vivid mind focusing on great ideas that move or help people.

3. Social-Futurist-Feeler-Adapter: "The Communicator." Able to get into the skin of others. Inspires others to action. Never a dull moment.

4. Internal-Futurist-Feeler-Adapter: "The Poet." Cares about feelings and emotions. Easy-going manner. Deep feelings and thoughts on life issues.

5. Social-Futurist-Thinker-Planner: "The Executive." Seeks leadership. Gets things done. Moves forward with the plan and people like it.

6. Internal-Futurist-Thinker-Planner: "The Visionary." Self-assured and does it big. Makes big decisions and builds systems to fulfill the dream.

7. Social-Futurist-Thinker-Adapter: "The Entrepreneur." Renaissance person interested in everything. Sees possibilities. Breaks the mold.

8. Internal-Futurist-Thinker-Adapter: "The Analyst." Thinks and communicates with accuracy. Sees subtle similarities and differences. Analyzes the world.

9. Social-Realist-Thinker-Planner: "The Manager." Sees where things are and what needs to be done. Works with others well. Steady and dependable.

10. Internal-Realist-Thinker-Planner: "The Technician." Works with machine-like regularity. Keeps systems running. Better with things and ideas than people.

11. Social-Realist-Feeler-Planner: "The Schmoozer." A social animal. Creates feelings of harmony and goodwill. Likes to entertain.

12. Internal-Realist-Feeler-Planner: "The Guardian." Wants to be helpful to others. Protects the system. Has very high sense of tradition and institutional loyalty.

13. Social-Realist-Thinker-Adapter: "The Negotiator." Wins trust and working relationships. Enjoys competition. Will use shock effect to make a point.

14. Social-Realist-Feeler-Adapter: "The Star." Attracts others with their entertaining personality. Smooth, witty, charming, and clever. Very generous.

15. Internal-Realist-Thinker-Adapter: "The Biker." Likes risk and adrenaline highs. Good with tools. Is romantic about life and freedom. Focused on action.

16. Internal-Realist-Feeler-Adapter: "The Connoisseur." High sensitivity to beauty and pleasure. Physically and artistically expressive.

Now, go to Appendix A and write the name of your temperament combination in your personality temperament box. You will write in the combination name like

"Manager" or "Visionary." Also, there is a place for "key themes." As you were going through your personality temperament discovery, one or a couple of key themes may have struck you as important. Briefly jot down what they are.

For example, you may have scored exceptionally high, like a 90% or 100%, on one or a couple of the characteristics. They are major themes in your personality. Or, a part of the description of your combination may strike you as very important and true. Or, you may have lined up totally on the left or right sides of the temperament scales. That is a key theme. Or, a descriptive word under one of your characteristics may have really stuck in your mind and explained why you act the way you do. Make a note of it in your Personality Temperament Box on your PLM worksheet in Appendix A.

Congratulations! You have just finished one of the most detailed and difficult parts of your Personal Life Mission Discovery. This section was tough, but the information is going to give you a lot of insight into your life's purpose.

This first section gives you an idea of why you do the things you do and why you like (or dislike) the things you do. For example, one woman who took the test discovered why she struggled so much with a particular co-worker. She discovered that she is a Communicator, a social-futurist-feeler-adapter. Her co-worker was a Technician, an internal-realist-thinker-planner. His personality was different at every step. It's no wonder that they very rarely see eye-to-eye on an issue, or that they have trouble agreeing on how to solve a problem. Her insight into her own personality helped her to see that her co-worker wasn't trying to create problems, nor did he dislike her or want to undermine her. They simply had different views because they were different "stews."

Like a hammer in a toolbox, personality temperament discovery is the fundamental tool in establishing your Personal Life Mission. But a toolbox with nothing in it but a hammer is ineffective. You can't loosen a nut with a hammer! In the next chapter, you will discover your people style and add another tool to your toolbox.

Chapter 3

Discovering Your People Power:
How You Make Your Mark

"Hang on to whatever it is that makes you unique
Because without it, you are just a big yawn."
Bette Midler

"I always wanted to be somebody,
but I should have been more specific."
Lily Tomlin

I'll Take Your Job, Thank You

When Hap Klopp (1994) was asked during a job interview at a clothing company what his one-year goal would be, his response to the interviewer was, "To have your job." Hap did not last long at that company. He then founded The North Face Outdoor Clothing Company. Hap's interview response and later actions showed his People Power in action. He was destined to either rise to the top where he could have control or to form his own company where he would have it. Some people need control, others need to persuade, some need to cooperate, and others need to do things right. Most of us need some combination of these and our combination makes us unique in our relationships with others.

How You Make Your Mark

We are social beings. We have to get things done either with people, through people, or we have to go around them to get it done. The second part of "wiring" that makes us who we are is how we make our mark through, with, or around people. That is a nice way of saying it. A more realistic way of saying it is that your People Power is how you get your way. That can sound selfish, but we all need to get our way to a degree to make our mark in the world.

W. Schultz (1958) in his research developed a theory of interpersonal behavior called FIRO (Fundamental Interpersonal Relationship Orientation). That theory presents three ways people relate to others. The first area is through inclusion. Schultz said people want to be included and they want to include others. The second area is control. People want to be controlled to some degree by others and to some degree they want to be in control of others. The third area is affection. People want to give and receive affection. Schultz went as far as to say people need these experiences with others in some combination to maintain sanity.

The FIRO theory was a seminal idea about how people relate to people. The People Power concept advances the thinking about interpersonal relationships. We agree with Schultz in that when people cannot relate to others by the combination of ways they need, it drives them nuts. It may not drive people to insanity, but it does drive people to change their lives.

Your People Power Is Your Natural Way of Impacting Others

Remember, your Personal Life Mission says what you do for whom. You have a unique impact that no one else can have. You are "called" to have that impact on a target of certain people. Your People Power will be a major piece of your personal puzzle that will give definition to what you do and for whom you do it.

48

Personality Temperament is how you relate to your environment. It is the most general view of your wiring. Your People Power is how you relate to people. This is a more specific piece of your wiring that you need to know.

Your People Power Style Defines Your Effectiveness and Energy

It is critical to understand your People Power style, because it defines your effectiveness and your energy level. You accomplish your goals best when you can relate to others through your People Power style that is your natural, inbred, wired mode of effectiveness. You do have to adapt your style for certain situations to be effective, but your overall working dynamics with others is most effective when you can fulfill your People Power style. Your Personal Life Mission is going to involve doing some things for some people in a manner that fits your People Power style.

When we are prevented from living and working in a way that allows us freedom in our People Power style, our emotional energy is drained. We become frustrated, angry, and depressed. On the other hand, when we can pursue our goals through our People Power style, we become optimistic and energized.

Your Personal Life Mission will have some frustrating challenges. Everything in life that is worthwhile comes through hard work. But it will include a general approach to living and working that will keep you energized for your best accomplishments by staying in line with your People Power style.

There Are Four People Power Styles

The Controller seeks to be in charge.

The Persuader seeks to convince others.

The Facilitator seeks harmony and benefit.

The Perfectionist seeks to do things right.

Most people have a dominant style. If they cannot accomplish their goals through their dominant style, they will attempt to do so through the other styles in some natural order. This combination of your dominant style and the order in which you will attempt the other styles is a big, big piece of who you are.

The next few pages will be the People Power part of the Chemistry Match™.

Discovering Your People Power Style

For each statement or question below, circle the letter of the response that best represents you most of the time.

1.   You generally are…

    A. Self-reliant and independent.
    B. Enthusiastic and motivating.
    C. Stable and cooperative.
    D. Conventional and analytical.

2.   You generally are…

    A. Assertive and directive.
    B. Charming and humorous.
    C. Patient and observant.
    D. Perfectionistic and precise.

3.   You would describe yourself as…

    A. Competitive, pro-active, or somewhat aggressive.
    B. Influential, pro-active, and convincing.
    C. Amiable, helpful, and loyal.
    D. Conscientious, responsible, and loyal.

4.   You generally appear to be…

     A. Self-assured, confident, and opinionated.
     B. Generous, open, and encouraging.
     C. Non-demonstrative and team-minded.
     D. Analytical, dependable, and correct.

5.   You consider yourself to be…

     A. Decisive and in control.
     B. Sociable and gregarious.
     C. Deliberate and steady.
     D. Focused with high standard of proficiency.

6.   You are…

     A. A risk-taker and independent.
     B. Trusting and positive.
     C. Territorial and cooperative.
     D. Courteous and unchanging.

7.   You like to think of yourself as…

     A. Forceful and dynamic.
     B. Emotional and motivating.
     C. A team player.
     D. Systematic and sequential.

8.   You are more…

     A. Controlling and directive.
     B. Impulsive and spontaneous.
     C. Predictable and steady.
     D. Diplomatic and analytical.

9.   You feel you are…

     A. Daring and courageous.
     B. Persuasive, humorous, and engaging.
     C. Loyal, objective, and responsible.
     D. Logical, level-headed, and right.

10. You are…

       A. Direct, forward, and goal-oriented.
       B. Gregarious, charismatic, and lively.
       C. Patient, cooperative, and steady.
       D. Accurate, credible, and stable.

Total the number of As, Bs, Cs, and Ds that you selected and place them below.

       A. Controller   %_____

       Enjoys controlling, overseeing, and being in charge.

       B. Persuader   %_____

       Uses persuasion and the art of promoting ideas to get people to come around to their thinking.

       C. Facilitator   %_____

       Likes to work within existing systems and policies to accomplish tasks (and wishes others would do the same).

       D. Perfectionist %_____
       Prevents trouble by doing the present task with perfection.

Now transfer these totals to your People Power Box on your PLM worksheet in Appendix A.

The Four People Power Styles and Their Combinations

Controllers Take Charge

Controllers take charge to overcome challenges. They feel a certain "rush" of excitement when they are faced with a problem or challenge that is going to require courage and decisiveness.

Controllers usually move about in the work place until they can find a situation that allows them the freedom to call the shots so they can "get it done now and get it done right." They seek high levels of responsibility and freedom to do it their way. Some even need to be the key leader of the organization or the owner of the business. Sometimes they say, "My way or the highway," to their employees. Some simply cannot work for others. They would rather work for themselves and have it tougher than to work for others and have it easier.

Controllers are seen as the most confident types. They seem to know where they are going and how they are going to get there. They are seen as the most aggressive type, and they are the least appreciated by the other three types.

Controllers have respect for other controllers but feel they are hardheaded and hard to work with. They view Persuaders as allies in getting things done, but also as people who talk too much. They view Cooperators as needing a lot of attention and passive. They view Perfectionists as obsessive about details.

There are Three Common Controller Combinations

1. The Organizer
   Typical Score: Controller   50%
                  Persuader   30%
                  Facilitator   0%
                  Perfectionist   20%

Aggressive, persuasive, active, and independent. A person of action, a self-starter who drives hard for goals regardless of what stands in the way. The worst thing is to give up; the last thing is to give in. A prime mover who loves competition. Prods, persuades, compliments, needles, exhorts or drives, depending on the situation. Enjoys power and responsibility. Pride drives to take risks and implement bold plans. Friendly to those on the team. Antagonistic to those who oppose.

2. The Dictator

Typical Score:	Controller	80%	or	70%
	Persuader	10%		0%
	Facilitator	0%		0%
	Perfectionist	10%		30%

Coldly aggressive, factual, and impatient. Driven to reach goals, even obsessive. Overcomes difficult problems with brainpower.

3. The Entrepreneur

Typical score:	Controller	40%
	Persuader	30%
	Facilitator	20%
	Perfectionist	10%

Aggressive, persuasive, and very independent. Supreme individualist who is cocky, energetic, and persistent. Incurable adventurer. Usurps authority and moves ahead without consultation or conference. Quick to react, quick to become bored and look for greener pastures. High sense of urgency and tolerance for pressure.

If you are a Controller, go to your PLM worksheet (even though you don't like being told what to do) and place the name of your combination in your People Power box, as well as any key themes you see. If you do not feel that one of the combinations adequately describes your Controlling style, go through the three combinations and highlight the characteristics you feel are descriptive of you. Write your own combination of key characteristics here:

_____

_____

What would you name your combination?

_____

_____

Persuaders Move Others

Persuaders strive to make their views and beliefs prevail. They are usually outgoing, persuasive, and gregarious.

Persuaders are interested in people. They are easily met, conversationalists who can sell themselves. They enjoy meeting new people and usually have a wide range of acquaintances.

Persuaders intuitively have a sense for the things that influence the opinions and ideas of others. They can be logical, humorous, charming, hurt, forceful, witty, and many other things depending on what it takes to win someone over. They can weave a story with the purpose of getting others to buy into their program. They often dress for success, being very aware of how their dress impresses others. They often are motivated to have status symbols as means of gaining credibility and influence. They join groups for status, prestige, and influence.

Persuaders are energized by recognition. If a Persuader's boss or superior gives ample rewards, credit for accomplishments, and recognition, that person will give them their loyalty.

Persuaders manage people in a very optimistic way. They work best for a democratic supervisor who is as much a friend as a boss.

One way to frustrate a Persuader is to not listen to him or her. The Persuader usually feels that if she can get her foot in the door, she can make the sale or win the job or get the approval she is seeking.

Persuaders are driven to get others to listen to them and see things from their point of view. Those who listen become friends, and those who do not, do not.

There are three common Persuader combinations.

1. The Motivator
   Typical Score: Controller   30%
                   Persuader   50%
                   Facilitator   0%
                   Perfectionist   20%

Outgoing, on the move, independent, and verbally aggressive. A social animal. Likes to play but knows when to work. Business and leisure involve people. Friendliness is used for results. Charismatic and can be agreeable even when disagreeing. Stands up for what is right. Can laugh at self and tries not to intentionally hurt others.

2. The Diplomat
   Typical Score: Controller   10%
                   Persuader   50%
                   Facilitator   10%
                   Perfectionist   30%

Enthusiastic, modest, active, and diplomatic. Tactful, cheerful, and at home with strangers. Dispels gloom with words. Smooth and low pressure "sales" talk. Good at small talk and easily starts conversations. Maintains a pleasant atmosphere of goodwill. Smooth and at home with a large circle of friends and associates. A good politician who knows the value of a well-stocked rolodex.

3. The Promoter
   Typical Score: Controller   30%
                   Persuader   50%
                   Facilitator   20%
                   Perfectionist   0%

A direct-action extrovert who is goal-minded and self-motivated. Thrives on taking risks. Friendly but argumentative and persistent in the pursuit of goals. Talking is more important that listening. Dominates social and work settings. Gets to talking and things pop into their heads and out of their mouths. Can bluff convincingly that they know about most subjects.

If you are a Persuader, go to your PLM worksheet (even though you would rather talk about it) and place the name of your combination in your People Power box, as well as any key themes you see. If you do not feel that one of the combinations adequately describes your Persuading style, go through the three combinations and highlight the characteristics you feel are descriptive of you. Write your own combination of key characteristics here:

_____

_____

What would you name your combination?

_____

_____

Facilitators Help Others Succeed

Facilitators are the oil that lubricates a system, an organization, or a business to keep it running smoothly. They keep things in order and harmony.

Facilitators are the keepers of traditions. They dislike change just for the sake of change. If a change is necessary and they believe in it, facilitators will become hard workers to try and make it work.

Facilitators are energized by fulfilling the key roles that make a system work. They are team players. They want others to be team players. They sense intuitively the power of what is accomplished when everyone does their job in harmony toward the same goal. They take pride in having their area of responsibility well covered and under control.

Facilitators usually work best in an existing system or with someone they believe in who takes the risks in establishing a system. They usually do not feel the urge to start a business themselves if they can find an existing business or organization where they can play a key role that is fulfilling.

Facilitators thrive on clear and regular feedback, which lets them know if they are doing what really needs to be done. They are frustrated when management leaves them in the dark about their performance. They would rather have a bad report, than no report so they can adjust and do well.

Facilitators are the cooperators, enablers and harmonizers of families, neighborhoods, businesses, and organizations.

There are three common Facilitator combinations:

1. The Specialist
   Typical Score: Controller   0%
                  Persuader   10%
                  Facilitator   60%
                  Perfectionist 30%

Quiet, amiable, and self-controlled. Maintains familiar routines and keeps a few relatively close friends. Cool-headed, reflective, and considerate. Proceeds at a deliberate pace. Can plod through tough jobs to get them done. Consistent, steady, and practical.

2. The Investigator
   Typical Score: Controller   50%
                  Persuader   0%
                  Facilitator   50%
                  Perfectionist   0%

Determined, logical, tenacious, and rigidly independent. Decisive, deliberate and will share opinions. Enjoys following leads, chasing clues, digging for facts, and uncovering hidden meanings. Analyzes problems and evaluates circumstances objectively and dispassionately. Wins with patience, getting results without a sense of urgency. Excels with long, hard work rather than with flashes of insight or inspiration.

3. The Advisor
   Typical Score: Controller   0%
                  Persuader   50%
                  Facilitator   50%
                  Perfectionist   0%

Easy going, friendly, relaxed, and independent. A nice person who poses no threat and is hard not to like. Is seen as liking people and open to listening. People are drawn to this person by warmth, empathy, and understanding. Wants to share ideas to help others. Is self-confident and poised.

If you are a Facilitator, go to your PLM worksheet (it will help us out if you will) and place the name of your combination in your People Power box, as well as any key themes you see. If you do not feel that one of the combinations adequately describes your Facilitating style, go through the three combinations and highlight the characteristics you feel are descriptive of you. Write your own combination of key characteristics here:

_____

_____

What would you name your combination?

_____

_____

Perfectionists Do Things Right

Perfectionists do things right or they don't do them at all. They make their mark in the world by their precision and correctness. They become known for their accuracy.

Perfectionists do not have People Power so much by their people skills as by their skills at doing their "thing" right. They are detail-oriented and seek to know what they are talking about.

Perfectionists focus on things they can do well. They avoid pursuits where they do not have the skills or knowledge to excel. That only causes frustration. They seek situations where they have the right amount of resources and lead time to get things done properly. Perfectionists in business often advertise that they are the best at their craft or that they do it right the first time.

Perfectionists find great pleasure at looking at their work and seeing that they have done it well. They are very frustrated by their own mistakes and failures. They can be unforgiving of themselves and sometimes of others, too.

They chafe in a job where they are not given the resources and the time they need to get the job done right. They struggle with management that pushes them too fast without having their ducks in a row.

The perfectionists of the world give us the products, ideas, and systems that come from intense attention to detail and accuracy.

There are three common Perfectionist combinations:

1. The Adaptor
Typical Score: Controller   0%
               Persuader   0%
               Facilitator   40%
               Perfectionist 60%

Conservative, reserved, stable, and conscientious. Cooperative, compliant, systematic, and courteous. Follows procedures and lives up to high standards. Sensitive and alert to possible danger. Looks ahead to avoid unnecessary trouble. A passion for impeccability and order. Follows directions precisely to turn in an error-free performance.

2. The Creator
Typical Score: Controller   40%
               Persuader   10%
               Facilitator   10%
               Perfectionist 40%

Forceful, factual, impulsive, and systematic. Often highly intelligent with a look of disorganization. Thinks in terms of concepts, theories, and probabilities. Investigates thoroughly and pursues all possible solutions to a problem. Can't accept any answer, must have the answer. Creative and perfectionistic.

3. The Stickler

Typical Score:		
Controller	10%
Persuader	0%
Facilitator	10%
Perfectionist	80%

Reliable, logical, alert, and accurate. A stickler for system and order. Decides by proven facts. Meticulously lives up to high standards. Tries to avoid unnecessary trouble. Uneasy until the correctness of actions or decisions is confirmed. Sensitive to hidden meanings and ulterior motives. Conservative and foresighted.

If you are a Perfectionist, go to your PLM worksheet (and get it right, please) and place the name of your combination in your People Power box, as well as any key themes you see. If you do not feel that one of the combinations adequately describes your Perfectionistic style, go through the three combinations and highlight the characteristics you feel are descriptive of you.

Write your own combination of key characteristics here:

_____

_____

What would you name your combination?

_____

_____

A summary way to help you think about the different People Power styles is the following matrix:

The Four People Power Styles and Their Preferences

Preferences	Controllers	Persuaders	Facilitators	Perfectionists
Natural Strengths	Takes Charge Results focused Confident Courageous	Communicates Relates Enthusiastic Convincing	Reliable Dependable Needs focused Peacemaker	Accuracy Attention to detail Reliable Competent
Natural Weaknesses	Impatience Inflexible Insensitive	Disorganized Wings it Over reaches	Gets used Stays quiet Doesn't initiate	Demanding Forgets people Critical
Likes	Challenges Options Clear answers	Status People Big picture	Appreciation Clear expectations Consistency	Time to prepare Organization Cleanliness
Dislikes	Losing Control	Criticism	Conflict	Incompetence
Playground	"We will play this game or I will take my ball and leave"	"We should play this game because..."	"Let's get along"	Only plays if it is a game they can play well.
Restoration	Physical exertion	Social Interaction	Doing nothing	Quiet organization
Money	Power	Influence	Consensus	Facts
Bumper Sticker	Lead, follow or get out of the way	Want to earn $500 in your spare time? Call 555-5555	Live and let live	Do it right the first time!

Congratulations! You have now completed two major pieces of your PLM puzzle. Personality Temperament and People Power are major pieces of God's writing on your life.

Before proceeding to chapter four, reflect on how the two pieces you have discovered so far relate to each other. What do you see about your Temperament combination and People Power? How do your Temperament and People scores appear to be saying similar things about you? How do your Temperament and People scores appear to be saying opposite or at least different things about you?

Triangulation

John's fishing hole on the ocean in Mexico is a place where he has gone since he was a kid. There is a deep reef there that has been known to produce some great red snapper and rock bass fishing. Before the days of global positioning systems, the way they would find the reef was by triangulating off some reference points along the coastline. By lining up the mountains like gun sights at two points along the cost, their boat was positioned at a third point, making a triangle. When the gun sights lined up, they knew they were over the reef. It was time to fish or cut bait.

As we go through the third piece of your wiring, we are tapping the power of triangulation. We are lining up three reference points of your personal inner design. It helps gain accuracy.

The third piece is your Project Zone. In chapter four, you will complete the triangle of understanding your wiring. You will gain a sense of personal position in the world. As you see you Personality Temperament, your People Power, and your Project Zone line up, you will understand better the time and place when you must fish or cut bait.

Chapter 4

Discovering Your Project Zone: The Zone You Own

"I used to work at The International House of Pancakes.
It was a dream, and I made it happen."
Paula Poundstone

"You've got to be very careful if you don't know where you are going,
because you might not get there."
Yogi Berra

I Was Supposed to Be a Waiter

I worked as a waiter for the Four Seasons' Las Colinas Sports Club in Irving, Texas while attending graduate school. Being a waiter is pretty much a maintenance kind of job. You are fulfilling the expectations of the customers and restaurant system for whom you are working.

While I was employed there, the Four Seasons Corporation decided to expand the golf facilities to include a new Tournament Players Course in addition to its existing golf course. The club hosts the Byron Nelson Golf Classic every May, so the new course would accommodate the tournament well. That project intrigued me. I began to hatch an idea about a "relief house" that could be built on the backside of the course at the farthest point from the club house.

Playing golf in Dallas in the summer can be a very hot and draining experience. I developed an idea for a drive-through relief house where golfers could drive their carts right through the middle of it. It would be a brick building with a cart path through the middle. On the left would be a service counter where golfers could buy food, drinks, and basic golf supplies. On the right would be restrooms and self-service vending machines for low-traffic times when the concession was not manned. The drive-through would have cool air blowers for summer and space heaters for winter. The idea was a combination of several already existing ideas:

*   Drive-through fast food places

*   Relief houses on golf courses that were not drive-through

*   The cool air and hot blowers they have at theme parks or sporting events to keep people comfortable

*   The fact that this club had a reputation for excellent service amenities.

So I got on my little Macintosh computer and drew up a picture of what this relief house would look like. I drew a floor plan and a picture of some golfers going through it. One was saying to the other, "Man, your club has everything!" I packaged the idea and sent it to corporate headquarters in Toronto.

A month later at an all-employees meeting, the club CEO held up a copy of the relief house proposal he had received from headquarters and said, "This is the kind of contribution that makes this place great." When they built the new course, they also built a drive-through relief house. In fact, they said they planned to build them at several other facilities they had around the world including one in Hawaii.

I was supposed to be a waiter, but I ended up being a golf relief house designer. And I did it without pay. Why? Because my Project Zone is to be a "Developer," and I have to develop whether I am paid to or not. You have to fulfill your Project Zone whether you are paid to or not. In fact, in every job we have, we try to do it the way we are wired, regardless of how our job description says we are supposed to do it.

What zone do you own? When you discover your project zone it will help you do three things. It will help you find the kind of job where you naturally excel. It will help you find the right fit inside your current organization. And it will help you find an organization that is at the stage in its life that will motivate you.

The Five Project Zones

Conceiver--------Creator--------Developer--------Refiner--------Maximizer

Conceivers mentally wrestle with ideas, problems, and theories to find solutions and generate new ideas. They have a high flow of ideas. Symbol: light bulb.

Creators use existing ideas and materials to make new things. They make things work for the first time. Symbol: Trade Mark (TM).

Developers make existing ideas, products, or systems that work even bigger. They apply ideas seen in other successful models. Symbol: growth curve.

Refiners make good systems better. They improve products and organizations. Symbol: +.

Maximizers manage good systems for maximum efficiency. Symbol: Swiss watch.

The Five Project Zones and the Better Mouse Trap

The Conceiver wrestles with mouse trap theory and with the problems of why they don't work better.

The Creator goes to the drawing board or workbench to design a proto-type of a new mouse trap and sticks with it until it actually works.

The Developer packages and markets the new mouse traps and develops a system for making and selling a ton of them.

The Refiner makes the mouse trap or The Better Mouse Trap, Inc., better.

The Maximizer squeezes out the most quality or profitability by managing BMT, Inc., like clock-work.

Discovering Your Project Zone

For each question or statement below, circle the response that best represents you most of the time.

1. Imagine that you are involved in the building of a new house. Which one of the following activities would you most prefer to do?

      A.   Designing from scratch how the house will look.

      B.   Drawing some building plans from a collection of sketches or other drawings.

      C.   Taking the plans and getting construction started.

      D.   Making design and construction improvements.

      E.   Seeing that the project is done correctly, on time, and on budget.

2. Suppose you are given an opportunity to pick a project or activity that you would enjoy doing very much. Which of the following parts of that project would you most enjoy working on?

A.   Coming up with the idea.

B.   Making the idea actually work.

- C.   Making the idea work for you or in a bigger way.

D.   Making improvements and increasing the potential after the project is up and running.

E.   Taking charge of a good project and making it run with effectiveness, efficiency, and under control.

3. Which compliment would you most prefer to receive?

A.   You are brilliant, original, creative, and unique.

B.   You are not only creative, you make things work.

- C.   You can really take a challenge and make it happen.

D.   You make the things you touch better.

E.   You are a highly effective and efficient person.

4. Which of the following committees would you prefer to serve on the most for a big event?

A.   The Theme Committee.

- B.   The Program Committee that comes up with how to do it.

C.   The Promotion Committee that markets the event and gets people to come.

D.   The Steering Committee that oversees the whole event to be sure every angle is covered.

E.   The Event Committee that carries out the actual tasks, making sure that everything goes as planned.

5. Which is your most preferred approach to ideas?

   A. I like to explore theories and possibilities without having to make it happen.

   B. I like to make a theory or idea work for the first time, then I like to hand it off to others to implement.

   C. Once I'm convinced an idea works, I like to put the strategic things in place to really get it off the ground, then I like to hand it over to others to run.

   D. I like to take good ideas and make them better, then I like to turn them over to others to manage.

   E. I like to take successful ideas and manage them for on-going success.

6. What part of a group vacation would you want to contribute?

   A. Come up with a new idea of where to go and what to do.

   B. Plan how to get there and what to do.

   C. Set up who is going to do what and where.

   D. Research the best ideas and how to get the most for our money.

   E. Being the trip manager, keeping everything on schedule so there are no loose ends or problems.

7. How long do you like to work on projects?

   A. Until the problem is solved in my mind.

   B. Until the problem is solved in practice.

- C.   Until there is growth and progress.

D.   Until its potential is reached.

E.   For a long time to achieve quality and dependability.

8. What would be your preferred contribution to an important product?

A.   Conceiving the idea.

B.   Making the first working model.

- C.   Growing the number of users and production.

D.   Improving the product or system after a period of field testing.

E.   Managing production.

9. What really frustrates you in a project?

A.   Not having freedom to come up with creative ideas.

- B.   Moving too slowly and staying with projects too long.

C.   Having obstacles blocking my goals.

D.   Seeing wasted potential.

E.   Seeing a lack of control and a waste of resources.

10. What would be the best job for you in a large advertising business?

A.   Coming up with new ideas.

B.   Designing artwork, ad copy, and strategies.

C.   Consulting new clients on the best advertising methods used by others that

could apply to their needs.

D.   Coming up with ways to improve the advertising of existing clients.

E.   Managing accounts, personnel or finances.

Add up the total number of As, Bs, Cs, Ds, and Es and place them below.

A:	Conceiver	10	0%
B:	Creator	20	0%
C:	Developer	60	0%
D:	Refiner	10	0%
E:	Maximizer		0%

Now go to your PLM worksheet and place your percentages in your Project Zone box.

Your Project Zone Range

Your Project Zone Range is how far across the zones your scores spread. Some have scores evenly spread all the way across the zones. Some "stack" 100% in one zone.

If you spread across zones, it shows that you maintain motivation to work throughout that range of zones. If you stack in one or two zones, it says you prefer to specialize.

Your Motivation and De-motivation

You become motivated at the zone in a project where your first score starts. You become de-motivated at the point where your score runs out.

If you've ever observed a relay race, you know that each leg of the race requires athletes with particular abilities. The first runner needs to be the most explosive, quick off the starting block, and driven to get out in front as early as possible. The second and third runners must be coordinated at taking the hand-off of the baton and carefully timing their starts so as not to leave too early or too late. Without careful timing, the baton is dropped — race lost. The final athlete, or "anchor," is usually the one who responds best to the pressure of the final lap, knowing that the race may be his to win or lose.

Which "leg" or phase of a project do you prefer to work on? Do you like to be in on the start of things, when people are still talking about ideas and possibilities? Or are you better suited to something that is up and running, where the expectations are clear and the circumstances are well-defined?

This motivation is a natural part of your wiring. You have to fulfill it. And you are at your best when you are naturally motivated. It's important to know when and where you are motivated and where and when you become de-motivated. Otherwise, you are liable to feel bored or frustrated, or you are liable to bore or frustrate others, because you are out of step with the race.

Note your range, motivation, and de-motivation on your PLM worksheet.

Your Project Zone

The Conceiver   Symbol: Light Bulb

The Conceiver is primarily fulfilled by discussing or thinking through the theoretical possibilities of a project, even if there is no need or possibility for practical application. The Conceiver likes to discuss the philosophical aspects of a concept or project, but leaves it to others to develop a working prototype, build it into a mature venture, and maintain it as an ongoing system. Conceivers are said to have "fertile" minds. The light bulb is always flashing.

The Creator   Symbol: Trade Mark

While Conceivers start from scratch, Creators start with existing ideas or materials and shape them into useable solutions. Creators make worthwhile ideas practical for the first time. The Creator likes to get an idea up and running to show it works, but then likes to hand things over to someone else to implement and maintain. The Creator role is a start-up role, and those who have it tend to get bored once they have to do the same thing over and over again.

The Developer   Symbol: Growth Curve

The Developer's motivation is to grow an idea in his or her own situation using a model of success seen elsewhere. The Developer thinks, "If it works in that situation, it should work in my situation." So the Developer is motivated by goals, quotas, and challenges duplicating the success of a prototype to a higher degree. However, the Developer gets bored with maintenance after the project makes its large strategic jumps and soon moves on to conquer new mountains.

The Refiner   Symbol: +

The Refiner is primarily fulfilled by reaching the potential of an existing product or service, shaping it into a system that is consistent and productive. Quality is the name of the game. As long as there is additional potential to extract from a person, program, or organization, the Refiner stays motivated. But once potential is reached, the Refiner loses interest and wants to hand things off to a manager.

The Maximizer   Symbol: Swiss Watch

The Maximizer is primarily fulfilled by organizing and controlling an already existing system. The goal is to maintain precision so that things operate smoothly, efficiently, on time, and on budget. For this reason, the Maximizer is wary of change or risk that could upset the delicate task of making things run the way they "should." Maximizers are often in it for the long haul and pride themselves in a long, spotless record.

You Have Had Your Project Zone for Awhile

Remember when we said that your personality temperament was how you were wired? Just as personality doesn't "happen" overnight, it is something you're born with, so too your People Power and Project Zone. People will try whatever means they can to accomplish tasks in their zone, with their people power. If you look back over the course of your life, even in your earliest years, you can probably find examples of working in your project zone.

Exercise: Write down a couple of examples from your childhood or teen years where you can see how you were working in your Project Zone.

_____

_____

_____

Section I Summary: Your PT, PP, and PZ Wiring Triangle

Remember the idea of triangulation from the fishing example? Three points in navigation can place you in the right spot. Now think about the three points of your wiring: your Personality Temperament, People Power, and Project Zone. What word or phrase stands out in your mind as the concept you have learned about yourself in these areas? Write them below.

Your Present Wiring Triangle.

Personality Temperament:

People Power: **Project Zone:**

This completes the section on your personal wiring. Next we are going to look at your unique personal history. You were made unique in your personality but you also have walked a unique path in your life story. Both your personality wiring and your life experiences shape who you are and where you are going. Be sure to fill out your PLM Worksheet in the center Present Wiring Columns before moving on.

Now, let's look at your story.

Chapter 5

Discovering Your Life Highlights:
Strength From Joy

"I owe my success to having listened respectfully to the very best advice,
and then going away and doing the exact opposite."
G.K. Chesterton

"I once complained to my father that I didn't seem to
be able to do things the same way other people did.
Dad's advice? 'Margo, don't be a sheep.
People hate sheep. They eat sheep.'"
Margo Kaufman

My Pastor Was a Dad

Without warning, the air split from the sound of the rattlesnake. I jumped over it, but my dad stopped instantly. My heart pounded and my legs shook. "Here," Dad said, and tossed me a shotgun shell. I was ten years old, and, like Barney Fife, only allowed to carry my gun unloaded. I loaded it, aimed, and squeezed the trigger. The shot severed the snake's head, and the rattling slowly faded to silence.

Today that rattle sits in my cigar box with other treasures from my past. It reminds me of a great day in the field with my dad.

I value that experience and many others like it for the values they instilled in me. I was a pastor's kid and had many experiences in religious activities, but the things that instilled the most values in me were the "non-religious" experiences with my dad. I know a lot of pastors' kids. They usually say, "My dad was a pastor." My experience was that my pastor was a dad. And that was one of my greatest life-shaping experiences, having a great dad.

It makes me who I am. One of my core life messages is for fathers to take advantage of the window of opportunity they have to spend time with their children. It can be the most powerful way to instill values in them.

My dad loves the ocean, as did his dad, and he began deep-sea fishing in Mexico when I was six. He began taking me along when I was eight. It was an adventure to haul trucks, boats, tents, and enough food and water to last ten days on a desolate Mexican beach. That special world he created once or twice a year during my window years affected me deeply.

Those Mexico trips usually occurred during the school year. Dad would take me out of school for up to two weeks to go with him. That might surprise some parents, but the reward was tenfold compared to what school could produce.

On return I came bearing trophies that turned the boys green with envy: shark teeth, stingray stingers, scorpions, and one time a live Gila monster.

That special world my dad created and brought me into was wonderful. I have permanent scenes planted in my mind of pounding surf, snorkeling with sea lions, whales up close and personal, and schools of manta rays.

I recall one scene when the Mexican sun burst into flame as it began its descent into the sea. We were preparing to pull the boats out of the bay and secure them on their trailers for the long trip home.

"Let's troll the point one more time," Dad said. I was waiting to see whom he was speaking to. "Well, let's go." And off we went, just Dad and me.

I was behind the wheel; Dad already had his line out, pulling his favorite homemade lure in the water. I hugged the rocks jutting out from the point as tightly as I dared. Dad's reel began to scream. "Snagged on the rocks," we both thought. I slowed the boat down and pointed the bow toward the open sea.

When we came to a stop, the reel kept singing. "I've got one!" He fought it as the orange glow of the sunset lit his face with anticipation.

The beautiful calico grouper came up beside the boat, brilliant with color. I reached for the landing gaff, but the fish made a desperate lunge, threw the hook from its jaw, and disappeared into the depths. We both sat back stunned, bobbing on the waves. Stunned. We lost the fish but not the power of a great experience together.

Today I am a father with five children. Whenever I leave the house, whether it is to go to the hardware store or to go fishing or to play golf, the most natural reaction for me is to see which one of my kids can go with me. It's who I am.

Ripped Off!

We are products of our past experiences. The people, places, things, and events of our personal histories shape our lives. They steer us to where we will go.

When Steve was a boy, an event happened that left a mark on his life. Steve's family ran a business that catered to the summer vacationers who came to the lakes in Minnesota. A large part of their business was the sales of clothing from manufacturers like Pendleton.

One year Steve's family had received their stock of merchandise, and they were preparing to open for the Christmas sales season. Late one night about three weeks before Christmas, thieves backed a large truck up to the door of their store, broke in, and stole over forty thousand dollars worth of clothing and merchandise.

It was devastating because the police could not find out who did it; Steve's family did not have insurance to cover their losses; and their annual income was based on a heavy seasonal income. They were wiped out.

Steve's dad did two things. First, he contacted all his creditors and discussed the situation with them and assured them they would figure out a way to make good on their debts. Second, he called a family meeting to discuss a strategy for creating quick revenue and to plan for the future. In that meeting they decided there was one thing missing in that area that might create a fast stream of income: a fine-dining restaurant.

They changed gears, re-built one of their businesses as a restaurant, obtained approval from their creditors to re-stock the clothing store, and rebuilt a family business that was even more successful than before. Not only did they pay back all the creditors, but also Steve's father was able to make enough income from the new business venture to retire at age 55. A disaster proved to be the opportunity to make adjustments and succeed. When Steve recalls those events, he says it taught him a lesson. Whether you say you can or can't, you're right. Had they taken defeat, they would have been defeated. But they said they could succeed and they did.

Discover Your Best Experiences

You have already had some good experiences but few people consciously think through them to understand which ones were the best defining ones.

We are going to lead you through a process of discovery. It flows in three stages. First, you will pinpoint and list your best memories, experiences, or events and chart these memories according to life stages. Second, from this list you will choose which of these experiences or events are Defining Experiences. Third, you will select from the list of Defining Experiences the three which you consider your best "Milestone" experiences.

To stimulate your memory you can organize your thinking by two categories: life stages and kinds of experiences. The kinds of experiences are people, places, things, and events. Think through each stage of life you have had so far and spend some time going down memory lane to recall your best experiences. Fill in the blocks in the following worksheet. This process may take a whole day that you set aside. If you will pay the price in these details you will be collecting the pieces that will build the structure of your PLM.

Your Best Experiences Worksheet

My Best Memories of People, Places, Things, and Events.

Life Stages	People	Places	Things	Events
Preschool				
Grade School Years				
15-25 Years Old				
25-35 Years Old				
35-45 Years Old				
45-55 Years Old				
55+				

Discover Which of These Experiences Are the Most Defining

Good experiences are the beginning, but let's go further. You need to know which of these had an impact on making you who you are. The way to discover the impact or how *defining* the experiences were is to ask three things:

1) How did the experience shape my core beliefs about God, life, work, or relationships?

2) In what ways did the experience give me a deep motivation to accomplish something or to change something in my life?

3) How did the experience seem to develop my talents or abilities?

Did That Experience Form My Core Beliefs?

A core belief is an idea that has stuck with you ever since the time it was formed in your mind, and it affects your choices today.

For example, one person may have had a good family but for some reason it just did not shape his or her beliefs that deeply. But for another it may be very profound. Dr. James Dobson, the founder of Focus on the Family, frequently refers to the experiences of his idyllic childhood in a stable family environment as a key factor in shaping his core beliefs. Not only did that experience shape his beliefs, but he is also deeply motivated to challenge others with those beliefs.

Did That Experience Give Me a Deep Motivation?

A friend who is a screenwriter had a best defining moment that shaped her career. She had taken a couple of weeks off work to visit family in Florida. She borrowed a laptop computer, deciding to work on her first screenplay. For two weeks, she poured herself into the script, playing out each scene in her head as she walked on the beach, then writing it down. Kat said, "That was the best two weeks of my life. I was where I wanted to be, doing what I wanted to do. I can't imagine anything better." Those two weeks gave her a deep motivation to pursue her dreams, to have the life that she wants fifty-two weeks out of the year rather than just two weeks out of the year.

Did That Experience Develop My Abilities?

My experience as a preacher's kid was good--not just because my dad took me fishing, but because my church experience was good too. My dad was a good communicator and he provided me a living laboratory to learn how to speak to an audience. One of the key lessons he taught me about public speaking was to always illustrate a major idea or point with a concrete story. I used to watch the audience come alive as he would move from some abstract idea to some funny or interesting story. I still sense the dynamic of audience alertness. The best communicators tell the most common, interesting, and understandable stories to make their points. My abilities to speak were developed by having a good example and mentor.

You have some core beliefs that come from some experiences. They convinced you that certain things about yourself, others, God, and the world are true. You have some deep motivations. You do some things to this day because of a drive instilled in you by some good experiences. And you have some abilities that surfaced as a result of people and/or events in your life.

Use the following worksheet to make your notes.

These Experiences were defining for me because they:

Formed My Beliefs		Motivated Me		Developed My Abilities	
Experiences	Beliefs	Experiences	Motivations	Experiences	Abilities

Identify Your Three Best Milestone Experiences

Your challenge now is to identify from the list you just made the three best milestone experiences that have had the most positive impact on your life. A Milestone Experience is a turning point that changes your beliefs, motivations, and or abilities in a significant way. It is a life transition.

Billy Graham had a milestone experience when he attended a meeting as a teenager and heard the evangelist Dr. Mordecai Ham. His decision to follow Christ changed the whole direction of his life. Dr. Martin Luther King, Jr. had a milestone experience when he was exposed to the racial reconciliation teachings of Paul Tillich in seminary. He had another milestone experience in 1954 when a lady in the town where he was a pastor refused to give up her seat on the bus. When Rosa Parks was arrested in

Montgomery, Alabama, Dr. King engaged the Civil Rights Movement and never looked back.

Your Milestone Experiences may or may not be as dramatic as these, but they did change the course of your life. List your top three Milestone Experiences here:

My Best Milestone Experiences

1.	2.	3.

Now go to your PLM worksheet and fill in your "Life Highlights" box with your top three best defining experiences.

The Patterns and Trends of Your Life

This PLM box and the next one on your PLM Worksheet will help you see the patterns and trends of your life. This storyline of your past provides a direction for your future. The good can be leveraged for more good. The bad can also be leveraged for good. This is one of the great lessons from human capacity and God's grace.

We did this one first because it is emotionally the easiest one as you get used to doing this kind of thinking. Now it is time to move through what for many is the hardest part of this whole process, your worst experiences. We call them your Life Intersections.

Just a word of encouragement. This will be painful for some because it is looking at past pains squarely in the eye. But we promise you, there will be some excellent things that can come from this part of your life and some of the most important pieces of your

Personal Life Mission will flow from it.

No person has ever accomplished anything of significance without leveraging

pain. You have some pain from your past. Until now, it may have just seemed useless.

But it can be leveraged for gain through your Personal Life Mission.

Chapter 6

Discovering Your Life Intersections:
Power From Pain

> "What in the world would we do with ourselves
> if obstacles did not stand in the way?"
> H.G. Wells

> "Don't go around saying the world owes you a living;
> the world owes you nothing; it was here first."
> Mark Twain

> "Most people use hurt as a reason to stop. Then you truly are hurt; you hurt yourself —
> you keep yourself from attaining your heart's desire. You do that by stopping."
> John-Roger and Peter McWilliams

It Cost Me a Brother

"My dad's obsession with money cost me a brother," my friend said. He said that after I told him that I thought he had zero tolerance for people who sacrifice their true lives purposes to make more money.

His father's drive to make more money caused tension and strife in his family because his father was distracted from being a dad. His brother ran away from home to escape the feelings of abuse and neglect and was killed in an auto accident en route to California.

My friend has a message to tell: "Money is okay in its place, but do not sacrifice what is truly valuable in the pursuit of it." Actually his message is a little stronger than that. "If you miss your life's purpose because you are blinded by the single-minded pursuit of money, you're an idiot!"

That life-message, that core conviction, came from a very painful experience in his past. He is in his fifties and is still impacted by what happened in his past. Being able to overcome a limiting belief about the value of money and developing a healthy respect for how it can be used to benefit society and others has been one of my friend's greatest challenges in life.

The Joseph Factor

Remember our discussion of Joseph in the Bible in chapter one? This is one of the greatest rags to riches stories of antiquity. He was a young man who was betrayed by the ones he trusted most: his family.

Through time and divinely ordered events, Joseph rose from being a slave to being the CEO of the largest financial empire of his day, Egypt, Inc. He was in charge of allocating the resources of the only power that had resources during a great seven-year depression. He saved the empire from ruin and made it even stronger. He saved his family, which was the beginning of the nation of Israel.

The Joseph Factor is found in one of the most inspiring phrases in the Bible. "You meant it for evil, but God meant it for good." Joseph did not discount the evil he had experienced. Being betrayed and lied about and abused was evil. But Joseph saw a larger picture with God in it. He saw that God could even turn evil into good. And he did.

There is evil in your past. We do not discount it. And we do not pretend that we can just whitewash over your painful memories. But here is what you have to know. If you choose to seethe in bitterness and anger at those who hurt you or even at God himself, you will reap the rewards of bitterness which is a life that is wasted. If you choose to leverage the bad for good, you will gain a power that you never dreamed could be in your life. The heads and tails together give you a power that money can't buy.

He Broke His Femur in His Mother's Womb

Tim Hargrove, my associate in pastoral ministry, broke his femur in his mother's womb. That began a life of broken bones.

By the time Tim was thirteen years old, he had broken 42 bones. He had a bone disease that caused his bones to be brittle. The breaks caused him to live in casts or a wheelchair up to the age of thirteen. His mother could not even hold him when he was a baby because the slightest pressure would break his bones. He had only been walking two years before he was old enough to move off to college. The repetitive breaks caused Tim to lose thirteen inches of height, so that today he stands all of four feet eight inches tall.

Tim is an excellent motivational speaker. He has a life's message and he has the abilities and convictions to communicate that message with power. His message is, "You are big enough to do whatever God wants you to do."

Tim's life is a living example of someone who has taken risks to advance his career and to be a powerful motivator of others. Tim was pressured by a sense of inadequacy as a kid in school because he was bound to a wheelchair. As he came into adulthood he was pressured by the feelings of inferiority for being not only shorter in height than men but most women, too. But Tim also sensed that God had a purpose for his life and for the evils he experienced.

Today Tim is looked up to by our church and many others as a spiritual leader and advisor to everyone who is seeking to overcome the struggles of life. A couple of years ago he moved to Vancouver to start a new church. The name of that church is the Pacific Rim Community Church and it is doing well. Tim also earned an advanced degree. Tim returned to our church staff where he leads some of our new and innovative ministries. He has learned to take good risks to produce good things.

I might add he has a pretty good golf game, too. I always get a kick out of teeing up with Tim and some new fellows who do not know us. I can imagine them wondering if he can hit the ball or not. He can, and often beats them!

Best Day/Worst Day

In the movie *City Slickers*, three friends who are on a cattle drive talk about their best days ever (when your kids are born is disallowed as being too easy) and their worst days. Ed, a man with significant relationship issues, talks about his best day. He was 15 and his mother had caught his father cheating on her again. Ed realized that his father wasn't just cheating on his mother but on the whole family. Ed tells him, "You're not good to us." When his father gets ready to hit him, Ed doesn't back away. His father just turns and leaves and never returns. Ed says, "But from that day forward, I took care of my mother and my sister. That was my best day." When asked what was his worst day, he replied, "Same day."

Very often, our worst days can become our best days because of how they shape us. Nietzsche said, "What doesn't destroy me makes me stronger." We have the choice. We can let our worst days destroy us or we can use them to make us stronger, to make us passionate people, and to spur us to create a better world. None of what you and I have encountered in this life has been by accident.

God knows our personal life histories from start to finish, just like he knows all of human history from start to finish. He knows prior to our births every situation we would encounter. God wastes nothing in life. Every experience has been allowed, if not directly authorized, by God. He has the incredible power to take even the painful areas of life and somehow turn them around to bring us to a better position.

Discover Your Worst Experiences

We will follow the same three-step process that we used in the last chapter. We will look at your worst experiences: we will see which ones were the most defining, and then we will see which ones are your top three Life Intersections. In the boxes below, think through your life stages and through the people, places, things, and events that you remember. What memories come back as the worst? This exercise is not about wallowing in the mud of self-pity. It is about honestly facing what we have been through, so we can build on the strength that can come from adversity.

My Worst Experiences Worksheet

My Worst Memories of People, Places, Things, and Events

Life Stages	People	Places	Things	Events
Preschool				
Grade School Years				
15-25 Years Old				
25-35 Years Old				
35-45 Years Old				
45-55 Years Old				
55+				

Which of These Worst Experiences Are the Most Defining?

Now it is time to place values on the worst experiences. By that we mean weigh how influential they were in making you who you are today. In order to go from the several, dozen, or several dozen worst experiences to a shorter list of the most defining, ask yourself the following questions.

Did That Experience Form My Core Beliefs?

Remember from the last chapter that a core belief is an idea that has stuck with you ever since the time it was formed in your mind, and it affects your choices today.

"I was raised in an orphanage," one client told me. "One day the older kids took me into the basement and put me in a trash can and sealed the lid so I couldn't get out." She had a phobic reaction and panicked. She thought she was going to die in there. That experience not only scared her at the time, but it set an idea in her mind that she has just been able to identify now that she is in her sixties. The core idea Dorothy carried in her mind was, "I am a piece of trash." That core belief has affected her actions all her life. She is just now learning to have freedom from insecurity caused by that false idea.

In fact, she has just discovered that she has an aptitude and a desire to do some writing. She has recently taken some writing courses. One book she aspires to write would be called *How to Get Out of the Trash Can of Life*. I hope she writes it; I want to buy the first copy.

Did the Worst Experience Give Me a Deep Motivation?

"I desperately wanted my friends to know my faith but I was greatly embarrassed to invite them to my church because it was so out of touch with their lives." That is the testimony of Bill Hybels, the one pastor in America who is most credited with creating the "Seeker Movement" in the church. He was motivated to create a church that would relate to the unchurched. The result was the explosion of Willow Creek Community Church into a congregation of over 20,000 in a suburb of Chicago. It also fostered a whole movement in existing and new churches who positioned themselves to be "seeker driven" or "seeker sensitive."

How old are you? What core motivations do you still carry today from the negative experiences that you wrote down?

Did the Worst Experience Develop My Abilities?

What can you do today that you would not have had the ability to do unless you had gone through a bad experience?

I went through mid-life crisis at age 28. That sounds crazy but my life and my self-image was so wrapped up in my career direction as a pastor that when I failed and my career crashed, so did my whole view of my life and myself. I was swimming in a pool of bad emotions and confusion. My poor wife lived with a real creep during that period. In fact, my sour spirit almost destroyed our marriage.

In desperation, I sought out Steve Johnson and he consulted with me on it. The information I learned about myself from my Profile assessments was revolutionary. It not only revealed to me why I had failed in certain areas, but it showed new areas I needed to pursue in my career and ministry to build on my strengths.

I became a Profile consultant myself because I was dealing with so many people who needed the same kind of direction that I got. Today I pastor a large church with many exciting ministries. I have the ability to deal with difficult leadership problems with success because of what I learned from my failure. I have a wonderful ministry of helping hundreds of other people discover their Personal Life Missions. This is fun, but I would have never had it without a bad experience. It may have been evil but God meant it for my good.

Write down any abilities you have gained from your worst experiences as well as the beliefs and motivations.

These Experiences Were Defining for Me Because They:

Formed My Beliefs		Motivated Me		Developed My Abilities	
Experiences	Beliefs	Experiences	Motivations	Experiences	Abilities

Identify Your Top Three Life Intersections

"My life mission," Susan said, "is to influence and encourage women to understand their inner beauty and worth." Susan was a victim. She had been raped in the parking lot of a college campus, and she had repeated experiences of abuse by some men in her life. These experiences left her with no sense of personal value or value in God's eyes.

Over time and through some good resources, Susan discovered several things. First, she discovered that she did indeed have value in God's eyes. That was the basis for her valuing herself. Second, she discovered some abilities she has as a communicator and leader. She has good poise as a speaker and is good at organizing a group.

Susan has a ministry in our church as one of our lay pastors. She leads a women's group and she uses that forum to teach some vital principles of God's love and self-worth to other women who have been bruised by life and feel unlovable. Because of the collisions she had at her Life Intersections, she is able to help others.

What are your top three Life Intersections?

My Worst Life Intersection Experiences

1.	2.	3.

Go To Your Personal Life Mission Worksheet

Transfer your answers to your Personal Life Mission Worksheet. Enter the answers for your Life Intersections.

You have just completed what is the hardest part of this process for most people. This may have been emotionally difficult. But it can pay you back many times if you will leverage the battle scars from your Life Intersections for the strength they can also give.

Reflect on the Patterns and Trends of Your Life

Between your Personality Wiring and your Best and Worst Experiences, you have built quite a body of information about yourself. What patterns and trends are you seeing? What would you title your personal life story so far?

The value of discovering your patterns and trends lies in whether or not these patterns have been beneficial to you or destructive? Some of us keep repeating the same self-sabotaging behaviors. Seeing the patterns and trends can help us repeat the things that have been beneficial and cease the things that hurt us.

When Sherry was twelve years old a neighbor woman confronted her in her yard and said, "You are a terrible child!" This one Life Intersection began a pattern of thinking in Sherry's mind that she was a bad person. Other bad Life Intersections seemed to confirm to her that it was true and she was unlovable.

When she reviewed the patterns and trends of her life she was able to see this and to realize what a sabotaging affect it had on her. It had limited her career, relationships, and her ability to dream. She was able to get a new start where the bad from the past no longer sabotaged her future.

Are there patterns and trends in your life that could inhibit your ability to accomplish your Personal Life Mission? Have you discovered a pattern you want to change? This may be a turning point in your life where you need to turn to God and ask his help in changing self-destructive behavior.

Be encouraged. God has been around all along. He has the ability to turn even the most inhibiting experiences and thoughts into something useful. He could have made you aware of it any time. But he is making you aware of it now. This could be your time. His desire is that you see what's going on in your life and find strength in him to embrace his mission for your life.

There is one more chapter in this section on Understanding Your Own Story. Chapter 7 is about your unique abilities or what we like to call Glimpses of Your Genius.

Chapter 7

Discovering Your Abilities: Your Glimpses of Genius

> "A musician must make music, an artist must paint, a poet must write,
> if he is to be ultimately at peace with himself."
> Abraham Maslow

> "The truth is that all of us attain the greatest success and happiness possible in this life
> whenever we use our native capacities to their greatest extent."
> Dr. Smiley Blanton

> "The Lord said…I have chosen Bazalel…and I have filled him with the Spirit of God,
> with skill, ability, and knowledge in all kinds of crafts—to make artistic designs
> for work in gold, silver, and bronze, to cut and set stones,
> to work in wood, and to engage in all kinds of craftsmanship."
> Exodus 31: 1-5

The Father of Modern Management Wasn't a Manager

Here's a contradiction. The father of modern management, Peter F. Drucker, is not a manager. He says so in his memoirs, *Adventures of a Bystander* (1991). But Peter Drucker does know his key ability. His focus has not only created a phenomenal career but has influenced thousands, including us, with basic philosophies of management.

So what is Mr. Drucker's key ability? If he has not been a stellar manager of Fortune 500 companies or an entrepreneurial phenomenon with franchises all over the country, what is it that he does best? Why do thousands of business and public leaders flock to his presentations and line their shelves with his books?

"I have always been able to ask the right questions," Drucker says. "I may not know the right answers, but I know the questions to ask and I ask them."

This is what Drucker has done as a reporter, economist, management consultant, and political and social commentator. That is why his memoirs are called the adventures of a bystander. He was not the business leader, the political leader, or the social leader. He was the bystander asking the right questions so that leaders could get a clearer perspective on their work.

"Focus your energies where excellent performance can produce extraordinary results." That is one of Drucker's rules of management. "Build on islands of strength" is a corollary. Peter Drucker did these personally by being a stellar asker of the right questions. The results of his life have been extraordinary in every field of endeavor where people must manage themselves and an organization.

Being an "extraordinary asker of the right questions" does not sound like a very prestigious ability. But Peter Drucker demonstrates the power in defining your abilities and focusing on them.

Most Carry a Shotgun, but Big Game Hunters Carry a Rifle

A shotgun shoots a handful of shot or BBs. The shot leaves the barrel of the shotgun and spreads out in a pattern. That gives a hunter the ability to take a bird in flight. It is effective for small game at close to medium range. A rifle shoots a single bullet with tremendous speed and accuracy. It is the gun for big game.

Your grasp of your abilities is like the gun you carry. It will define the size of the game you will bag with your life's efforts. If you want to take small game at close to medium range, it is okay to have a vague and general understanding of your abilities.

But if you want to take big game, if you want to accomplish extraordinary things with your life, you have to switch to a rifle. You get your rifle by clearly defining your top abilities.

Abilities Are Discovered in Past Proven Performance

Abilities, piece number six on your PLM Worksheet, are discovered in your past proven performance. This category does not deal with your potential. This is not a search of things that you might have a potential to do well but have simply not tried yet or had the chance to do. This search is for the things that you know you can do well because you have done them well. That is why this piece is in the My Design From My Past column of the PLM Worksheet.

Your Best So Far Will Probably Produce Your Greatest to Come

Your best ability in your past will be the key to your powerful future. This does not mean you will not pick up new skills and knowledge that will be important for the future. But it means that if you are an adult, your core ability that can leverage your greatest achievements has already been revealed. You just might not see it clearly.

A friend used to dream of performing musically. Stephen joined the band in school and soon became first chair trombone. He played in jazz band and thrilled the performances in front of a live audience. He wanted to learn to play guitar and so he taught himself. He knew that as an adult he wanted to be a performer. His abilities at that time were pretty clear. His parents, though, were less than thrilled. His father told him that all the musicians he had ever known had become drug addicts and ended up in prison. His mother encouraged him to go into management at a grocery store.

In other words, his vision became foggy. In time, he had a family and the vision became a little foggier as he struggled to provide for a growing family. Although the fog was thick, the vision was never totally obscured, and when Stephen had a couple of back surgeries due to his grocery store job, he had to quit. After floundering for a few months, he picked up his guitar and began giving guitar lessons. Then he found that he could perform. Now Stephen is happier than he has ever been. And he isn't on drugs!

Your greatest achievements have already revealed your abilities, but your vision, like Stephen's, might be foggy. Your job now is to clear the fog, see it, and name it. Once you have done that, you can line up your life to take advantage of it.

What If I Am Useless?

The fear that strikes some of us at this point is the worry that we do not have any abilities or that our abilities are useless. We fear we might be failures because we might be defective people.

The core abilities of some of the most influential and successful people in the world sound unassuming and frankly useless. "I make people laugh, I encourage people, I like math, I like to fix things, I love to dream up stories, I am curious how things work, I ask questions." These are some of the "useless" abilities of some of the most powerful people of history.

The most useless person is the person who does not grasp his or her abilities. No matter what package of abilities you have, if you will grasp them, you can leverage them for achievement.

Let's Look Back to Lift Some Fog on Your Abilities

We will work on defining your abilities in two ways. First, in this section, we will use a narrative approach. Second, in the next section, we will use an assessment approach. Both will help lift the fog concerning your abilities.

What Produced Your Best Results?

This sounds obvious, but many ignore it. You have to look back over your jobs, projects, interests, hobbies, and activities and ask what you did that produced the best results.

When I (John) was in school from elementary through college, I always did best on oral reports or presentations. When I saw I had the option of an oral presentation, I would look forward to it. The chance to get up in front of the class and speak, to make them laugh, and to make a point was great. Today I make much of my living as a public speaker. It is a key ability for me that has always been true. I have had to grow in my abilities and knowledge to be a good speaker, but the raw ability was already there.

When you look back, what has produced your best results? In school what served you best? In your jobs what has been your best stuff? Take a minute and jot down your thoughts in the space below.

Are You a People Person, a Thing Person, or an Idea Person?

A People Person's key abilities lie in relating to others. They accomplish the most through their relationships with others. My mother-in-law, Jimmie Nell, was an irrepressible People Person. I have never known anyone who was so connected with so many people around the world. She was connected to people through her and her husband's careers, her education, her hosting of exchange students, her political work, and her religious work. After we had traveled to another town, she would ask if we looked up so-and-so while we were there. When we would say "no," she would be incensed. She couldn't imagine not schmoozing with others when you have the chance. Many people have told us how she had a deep impact on their lives for good. Do you have great relationships? If so, that is a clue to your key abilities.

A Thing Person's abilities lie in the things they work on or with. They produce tangible products. They fix things. They make things. They build things. They love the things they specialize in. They like other people who have mutual interests with them in the same things.

Thing People like to touch, feel, observe, and appreciate the things they work with. Those things may be as low-tech as tomatoes or as high-tech as a laser generator. Thing People have made incredible advancements in the things that we enjoy in this modern age. And the things of the future will be developed, maintained, and fixed by those wonderful Thing People.

My father-in-law, Don, was a Thing Person. He was an engineer and he was great at fixing things. He led electronic and computer production teams for most of his career. He was a private pilot and he personally did the mechanical maintenance on his airplane that he flew in partnership with some other pilots. At one time Don owned two Mercedes Benzes and an old Porsche 914. Don tore the engines of all three of these German cars down to their blocks and rebuilt them. The man was a great thing person. It provided a good living for his family and the things he built have benefited society.

Then there are Idea Persons. Their abilities lie in their minds. They learn, analyze, conceptualize, theorize, and seek solutions. They love the world of ideas. They read to be in the playground of ideas. They like to be with others who like to work on similar ideas. They dislike being with others whom they perceive as "shallow." Sometimes Idea People are academics but other times they are very practical. Some Idea People come up with ideas that solve everyday problems. Some are NFL coaches. Some are preschool teachers. And many are frustrated in jobs where they have to be people persons or thing persons.

I am an Idea Person. I have good relationships. I also like to work with things like houses, cars, and boats. But my best work is with ideas. As a pastor I deal with many people personally in pastoral guidance and leadership. I deal with many things like budgets and facility development. But my greatest contribution as a pastor is in the world of ideas. My best stuff is in the ideas that fuel the vision for our church, the ideas that fill the sermons I preach, the ideas that drive the strategies of our ministries, and the ideas in the things I write to help others.

Are you a People Person, a Thing Person, or an Idea Person? What percentage do you feel you are in each? Write down what you think:

People Person _____ %

Thing Person _____ %

Idea Person _____ %

Are you in a career that takes advantage of your strongest characteristics? What would you say is your greatest ability in your highest category? For example, you might say, "I am a People Person and my greatest people skill is motivating people." Or you might say, "I am a Thing Person and my greatest ability is diagnosing why something doesn't work." Or you might say, "I am an Idea Person and my greatest ability is explaining complicated matters in simple ways."

Before moving to the next section, take a minute again to jot down some notes to yourself about your abilities. You will draw on them later to define your best abilities. Remember, this kind of work is going to earn you a rifle to take the big game of life.

When Did Others Affirm You the Most?

People affirm us in several ways. The most obvious way is verbally. People tell us that we did a good job or they express appreciation for what we did. Think about it. What has been the most repeated area of affirmation you have received in your life?

I (John) will always remember my junior high football coach asking me if I had any new jokes or stories. He said, "You tell the best stories." That stuck with me. I love to tell a good story. When I was engaged, my wife's sister and mother would read my letters to her. I knew they did, so I would write some outrageous things on purpose just to get to them. But they used to beg for more letters because they were so entertaining. These may sound off the wall, but they are part of one of the key areas of affirmation I have received throughout my life, and that is communicating stories.

"Imitation is the highest form of flattery." You have heard the saying. It is also a kind of affirmation. How have others imitated you? What is it about you they want to imitate that they see as good? That can give you a clue to your abilities.

Finally, how have others been changed or affected by you? What impact have you had on others? Whose life is better because of you, and how is it better? That can be a great clue to discovering your abilities. Write down your thoughts from this section.

What Gave You the Greatest Fulfillment?

We have a philosophy that your greatest fulfillment comes when you are doing what you are designed to do. Maybe not your greatest pleasure, but your greatest fulfillment. Pleasure is usually a short-term sensory experience. Pleasures are experiences like eating a piece of your favorite cake, taking a hot bath, catching a fish, or getting a hit in a softball game. Fulfillment, on the other hand, is a lasting and deep satisfaction that stays with you and keeps coming back.

What product, solution, system, accomplishment, or work have you done that you look back on with fulfillment? One of our friends is a building contractor in Texas. He says, "I love to look at the finished product and see what a dramatic change we have made by remodeling or from a new construction." Maybe performing on stage in sixth grade is a moment that has stuck with you. Maybe convincing others to buy a product or believe in something was fulfilling to you.

When my daughter, Carolina, was seven she showed signs of being a good salesperson. She took some old pieces of grout from a shower I had demolished and set up a stand in the front yard to sell them to the neighbors. Of course no one wants used grout, but she made some sales because she was so cute. She liked making the sale. Now she is a teenager and she still is competitive and persuasive. People are attracted to her.

Have you ever lost track of time? We believe that we are creatures with eternity written in our hearts. When we do things that are fulfilling to us, when we are in that groove that we were created to be in, we touch on that eternity and lose track of time. When did you lose track of time? We tend to watch the clock when we are doing unfulfilling work. When we are doing fulfilling work, we are shocked to see how much time has passed. What activities do you get so lost in that time flies? Write them down.

Your Top Three Abilities So Far

We have just come through a narrative section of self-discovery. Think about the following questions:

1)   What has produced your best results?

2)   Are you a people person, a thing person, or an idea person?

3)   When have others affirmed you most?

4)   What has given you the most fulfillment?

List your top three abilities as best as you can:

My #1 Ability _____

My #2 Ability _____

My #3 Ability _____

This narrative section has lifted the fog a little bit. It has helped you to understand some important things about you. The next section is going to be an assessment exercise to help you think through your abilities. It will bring your picture even more into focus.

Abilities Assessment

The following is the Abilities Assessment from the PathMaker™. It is made of

38 categories of abilities. Under each category are five specific abilities.

Go through all the abilities listed and rank each with an A, B, or C.

Rank an ability as an A if you *definitely* have that ability.

Rank an ability as a B if you think you *might* have this ability.

Rank an ability as a C if you *do not have* this ability.

The Abilities Assessment

Analysis/Conceptualizing

The ability to research, analyze, synthesize, and evaluate ideas to understand them better.

A B C

__ ✓ __ 1. Learn quickly by watching or listening to others, reading, observing or studying.

__ ✓ __ 2. Gain a quick grasp of concepts, different approaches, or new and different ideas.

__ __ ✓ 3. Understand complicated or technical instructions.

✓ __ __ 4. Read with good comprehension and speed.

__ ✓ __ 5. Study what makes things work the way they do, or study steps that enter into a process.

1 3 1 **Total checks for this category.**

Problem Solving

The ability to correctly diagnose the causes of problems, to find solutions, and keep cool under pressure.

A B C

__ ✓ _ 6. Find creative and unusual solutions to hard-to-solve problems.

✓ __ __ 7. Help other work through difficult problems, showing them a strategy to solve them.

__ ✓ __ 8. Brainstorm with others in a "think tank" environment to overcome obstacles.

__ ✓ __ 9. Use intuition to find new ways to solve problems.

__ ✓ __ 10. See problems as a challenge more than an inconvenience.

1 4 __ **Total checks for this category.**

Mechanical/Repair

The ability to apply mechanical principles to practical problems.

A   **B**   **C**

___ ___ ✓ 11. Improvise, trouble-shoot, and solve physical problems.
___ ___ ✓ 12. Understand how machines work.
___ ___ ✓ 13. Solve mechanical problems.
___ ___ ✓ 14. Read plans, blueprints, and schematic drawings.
___ ___ ✓ 15. Repair toys, motors, appliances, and machines.

___ ___ 5 **Total checks for this category.**

Artistic Expression

The ability to develop visually pleasing or interesting items through the use of colors and shapes.

A   **B**   **C**

___ ___ ✓ 16. Create visually appealing architecture, sculpture, photographs, paintings, or graphics.
___ ___ ✓ 17. Apply color, shape, and design well.
___ ___ ✓ 18. Design sketches, illustrations, or paintings.
___ ___ ✓ 19. Paint or draw with colors or black and white.
___ ___ ✓ 20. Create pottery, woodcrafts, metalwork, or handcrafts.

___ ___ 5 **Total checks for this category.**

Musical Expression

The ability to express one's thoughts and feelings through musical composition or performance.

A   **B**   **C**

___ ___ ✓ 21. Apply musical knowledge to write, compose, or select music.
___ ___ ✓ 22. Perform solo in front of an audience.
___ ___ ✓ 23. Play an instrument as part of a group.
___ ___ ✓ 24. Set your thoughts and feelings to music.
___ ___ ✓ 25. Entertain people with vocal or instrumental talent.

___ ___ 5 **Total checks for this category.**

Interpersonal Communication

The ability to guide others by reassuring them, giving clear direction, responding to needs, or effective confrontation.

A	B	C	
✓	—	—	26. Understand others, clarify misunderstandings and give clear guidance.
✓	—	—	27. Respond to others' needs and feelings.
✓	—	—	28. Address others' concerns effectively.
✓	—	—	29. Ask good questions effectively.
✓	—	—	30. Help others express their thoughts and feelings.
5	—	—	**Total checks for this category.**

Group Performance

The ability to give group talks, demonstrations, or performances in front of an audience with poise.

A	B	C	
✓	—	—	31. Make presentations to groups.
✓	—	—	32. Be an emcee at a meeting or ceremony.
—	—	✓	33. Act, perform, dance, or do comedy.
✓	—	—	34. Show poise in awkward situations.
✓	—	—	35. Speak to a crowd with short notice.
4	—	1	**Totals checks for this category.**

Creative Writing

The ability to paint people, events, or scenes in writing.

A	B	C	
—	✓	—	36. Describe people, scenes, and events in writing.
—	✓	—	37. Write promotional or advertising materials.
—	✓	—	38. Write stories, poems, or plays.
—	✓	—	39. Move people to feel and act through writing.
—	✓	—	40. Use language to paint ideas, scenes, and situations.
—	5	—	**Total checks for this category.**

Technical Writing

The ability to use accurate technical language to explain, direct, or summarize procedures and ideas.

A	B	C	
✓	—	—	41. Write clear concise reports, letters, and proposals.
✓	—	—	42. Accurately explain steps, procedures, and plans.
—	—	✓	43. Write instructions a reader can easily follow.
—	—	✓	44. Write a textbook, scientific or engineering paper, white paper, or other fact-based documents.
—	✓	—	45. Write complete sequential directions.
2	1	2	**Totals for this category.**

Teaching/Training

The ability to educate others by developing teaching strategies and delivering them to students.

A	B	C	
—	✓	—	46. Design a teaching plan or strategy.
—	✓	—	47. Create an interesting learning environment.
—	✓	—	48. Explain, instruct, or inform others on a new idea.
—	✓	—	49. Assess student's learning styles and tailor an approach to accommodate them.
—	✓	—	50. Follow a teaching plan and finish a course.
—	5	—	**Totals for this category.**

Data Handling

The ability to organize and process information so it can be easily retrieved.

A	B	C	
✓	—	—	51. File and store information in an organized way.
—	✓	—	52. Remember and apply detail accurately.
—	✓	—	53. Process data accurately.
✓	—	—	54. Organize and give information to the people who need it in a form they can use.
—	✓	—	55. Handle large amounts of computer/paper work.
2	3	—	**Totals for this category.**

Following Through

The ability to complete projects on time, on budget, and within quality requirements.

A	B	C	
__	✓	__	56. Finish projects when they aren't interesting.
__	✓	__	57. Follow instructions accurately.
✓	__	__	58. Complete projects on time and on budget.
✓	__	__	59. Fulfill tasks and return calls.
✓	__	__	60. Finding ways to increase efficiency.
3	2	__	**Totals for this category.**

Detail Observation

The ability to make accurate observations of surroundings or material things.

A	B	C	
__	__	✓	61. Find details in objects, pictures, or drawings.
__	__	✓	62. Detect small differences in a person's appearance.
__	__	✓	63. Detect small differences between nearly identical objects, numbers, shapes, or symbols.
__	✓	__	64. Notice typographical or grammatical errors.
__	✓	__	65. Find errors in computations or on receipts.
__	2	3	**Totals for this category.**

Office Machine Operation

The ability to operate computers, copy machines, faxes, adding machines, and cash registers.

A	B	C	
__	✓	__	66. Learn new computer programs.
✓	__	__	67. Use calculators and adding machines.
__	✓	__	68. Use sophisticated copy machines.
__	✓	__	69. Learn to use a new telephone system.
__	__	✓	70. Type more than 70 words per minute with less than 5 errors.
1	3	1	**Totals for this category.**

Financial Computing

The ability to perform arithmetic functions and to handle calculations with speed and accuracy.

A	B	C	
✓	__	__	71. Use numbers to solve problems.
✓	__	__	72. Count, compute, and analyze statistics.
__	✓	__	73. Understand and use mathematical concepts.
✓	__	__	74. Buy, sell, and manage money successfully.
✓	__	__	75. Do money calculations in your head.
4	1	__	**Totals for this category.**

Financial Management

The ability to manage money for yourself and others by planning, budgeting, and making wise financial decisions.

A	B	C	
✓	__	__	76. Plan, prepare, analyze, and administer budgets.
✓	__	__	77. Manage your and others' money.
✓	__	__	78. Use money to reach organizational goals.
✓	__	__	79. Control spending.
✓	__	__	80. Wisely saving and spending on the right things at the right times for the best results.
5	__	__	**Totals for this category.**

Promoting

The ability to influence others and persuade them to change their attitudes or ideas.

A	B	C	
✓	__	__	81. Influence others' ideas and attitudes.
✓	__	__	82. Persuade people to participate with you.
✓	__	__	83. Promote a new product.
✓	__	__	84. Campaign politically.
✓	__	__	85. Help others see the benefits in something.
5	__	__	**Totals for this category.**

Negotiating

The ability to resolve conflict or to create terms of agreement between people or groups for a good outcome.

A	B	C	
	✓		86. Negotiate or mediate a conflict resolution.
✓			87. Present opposing groups objectively and fairly.
✓			88. See the best win for all parties.
✓			89. Make peace.
	✓		90. Achieve compromise to preserve relationships.
3	2		**Totals for this category.**

Selling

The ability to convince others to buy.

A	B	C	
✓			91. Convince someone to buy something.
✓			92. Show how a product meets someone's needs.
✓			93. Win the trust and appreciation of others.
✓			94. Demonstrate the value of a product.
✓			95. Sense where a person is in a purchase decision and respond appropriately.
5			**Totals for this category.**

Independence/ Self-Management

The ability to initiate and complete work independently with little or no direction or supervision.

A	B	C	
✓			96. Work well without supervision.
✓			97. Initiate new work and relationships.
✓			98. Self-leadership in vision and purpose.
✓			99. Meet own budgets and plans.
✓			100. Control spending, time, and actions.
5			**Totals for this category.**

Initiating/Implementing

The ability to get things going and to get others going in a start-up venture or a new project.

A	B	C	
✓	—	—	101. Inspire others to follow your vision.
✓	—	—	102. Motivate others to achieve goals.
✓	—	—	103. Get others to use an idea you believe will work.
✓	—	—	104. Get the ball rolling on new projects.
✓	—	—	105. Create excitement for a new venture.
✓	—	—	**Totals for this category.**

Creating/Innovating

The ability to imagine and conceive new ideas, products, services, and solutions.

A	B	C	
—	✓	—	106. Invent new ideas or products.
✓	—	—	107. Conceive new ideas from random thoughts.
—	✓	—	108. Apply solutions from other fields.
✓	—	—	109. See new opportunities.
✓	—	—	110. Have a high number of ideas.
3	2	—	**Totals for this category.**

Strategic Planning

The ability to anticipate future needs, to create strategies to meet them, and to follow through.

A	B	C	
✓	—	—	111. See the future to structure the present.
✓	—	—	112. Lay out plans to be effective and efficient.
✓	—	—	113. Create a flow of tasks and resources working from the end product backward to the present.
✓	—	—	114. Evaluate strengths, weakness, opportunities and threats to understand strategic advantage.
✓	—	—	115. Understand strategy options and choose one.
✓	—	—	**Totals for this category.**

Supervising/Managing

The ability to manage others to meet organizational goals.

A	B	C	
✓	—	—	116. Be responsible for the output of subordinates.
✓	—	—	117. Select capable people.
✓	—	—	118. Assign the right work.
✓	—	—	119. Appraise subordinate effectiveness.
✓	—	—	120. Initiate removal of incompetent subordinates.
5	—	—	**Totals for this category.**

Leadership

The ability to acquire and sustain followers.

A	B	C	
✓	—	—	121. See new directions that need to be pursued.
✓	—	—	122. Inspire others to pursue a vision.
✓	—	—	123. Empower others to use their abilities.
✓	—	—	124. Model character and behavior for others.
✓	—	—	125. Encourage people.
5	—	—	**Totals for this category.**

Executive Leadership

The ability to give leadership at the top levels of an organization.

A	B	C	
✓	—	—	126. Predict social & cultural dynamics that impact the organization.
✓			127. Diagnose the fit between the environment and the organization.
—	—	—	
✓	—	—	128. Establish correct organizational structure.
✓	—	—	129. Lead the process of change.
✓	—	—	130. Wise decision making based on good information
5	—	—	**Totals for this category.**

Counseling/Coaching

The ability to help others understand themselves, their potential development, and encourage them in it.

A B C

A	B	C	
✓	—	—	131. Encourage others to learn more.
✓	—	—	132. Help others develop emotionally.
✓	—	—	133. Facilitate others' goal-setting.
✓	—	—	134. Help others develop their own insights.
✓	—	—	135. Help others turn potential into reality.
5	—	—	**Totals for this category.**

Empathy/Identification

The ability to see life through others' eyes and to patiently aid others in their situations.

A B C

A	B	C	
✓	—	—	136. See life through the eyes of others.
✓	—	—	137. Handle difficult or different people.
✓	—	—	138. Encourage people in hard circumstances.
✓	—	—	139. Gain trust and use it to help others.
✓	—	—	140. Feel what others feel.
5	—	—	**Totals for this category.**

Character Evaluation

The ability to correctly evaluate others' integrity, motives, and capabilities.

A B C

A	B	C	
✓	—	—	141. Sense a person's motives and attitudes.
✓	—	—	142. Assess the sincerity of others.
✓	—	—	143. See underlying problems others are hiding.
✓	—	—	144. Not be fooled by pretense.
✓	—	—	145. Evaluate the capabilities of others.
✓	—	—	**Totals for this category.**

Translating/ Cultural Understanding

The ability to accurately understand another language and/or culture.

A	B	C	
✓	—	—	146. Study and understand another language.
✓	—	—	147. Study culture to understand its significance.
✓	—	—	148. Relate to and appreciate another culture.
✓	—	—	149. Live in and be accepted by another culture.
✓	—	—	150. Interpret between two languages.
5	—	—	**Totals for this category.**

Cross-Cultural Relationships

The ability to build relationships with people of different, values, beliefs, cultures, and worldviews.

A	B	C	
✓	—	—	151. Speak a foreign language well.
✓	—	—	152. Able to be understood in a foreign culture.
✓	—	—	153. Accommodate the behaviors of people from different cultures.
—	✓	—	154. Motivated to relate to other cultures.
✓	—	—	155. Gain trust of people in other cultures.
4	1	—	**Totals for this category.**

Cross-Cultural Persuasion

The ability to persuade people from other cultures to hear, believe, and accept ideas different than their own.

A	B	C	
—	✓	—	156. Communicate new ideas effectively.
—	✓	—	157. Explain ideas that are culturally hard to understand.
—	✓	—	158. Convince a foreigner to adopt new ideas.
✓	—	—	159. Enjoy discussing different beliefs with others.
✓	—	—	160. Enjoy relationships with people of other cultures, values, and beliefs.
2	3	—	**Totals for this category.**

120

Hand/Finger Coordination

The ability to use your hands or fingers to do precise work or create products.

A	B	C	
—	—	✓	161. Use your hands to make a product.
—	—	✓	162. Use dexterity and hand speed.
—	—	✓	163. Fix or make small intricate products.
—	—	✓	164. Manipulate small objects with a steady hand.
—	✓	—	165. Use hand tools effectively.
—	—	—	**Totals for this category.**

Overall Coordination

The ability to apply physical effort and coordination to tasks with strength, endurance, and agility.

A	B	C	
—	✓	—	166. Extend yourself to your physical limits.
—	✓	—	167. Control total body movements.
—	✓	—	168. Physical coordination.
—	—	✓	169. Train to compete physically.
—	—	✓	170. Prepare for sports, dance, or combat.
—	3	1	**Totals for this category.**

Computer Skills

The ability to work with computers.

A	B	C	
—	—	✓	171. Understand computer hardware.
—	✓	—	172. Understand computer software.
—	—	✓	173. Troubleshoot computer problems.
—	—	✓	174. Build computers.
—	—	✓	175. Write software.
—	1	4	**Totals for this category.**

Cyber-Skills

The ability to create materials for and work with the Internet and cyberspace.

A	B	C	
__	__	✓	176. Build websites.
__	✓	✓	177. Repair websites.
__	✓	__	178. Install Internet systems.
__	__	✓	179. Create graphics and layout for web-sites.
__	__	✓	180. Develop web business sites and strategies.
__	1	4	**Totals for this category.**

Audio/Video Production

The ability to produce audio and video presentations.

A	B	C	
__	__	✓	181. Produce videos or films.
__	__	✓	182. Produce computer generated graphics.
__	__	✓	183. Run sound system for a concert or performance.
__	__	✓	184. Edit video.
__	__	✓	185. Produce music recordings.
__	__	5	**Totals for this category.**

Research

The ability to research ideas to discover new things.

A	B	C	
✓	__	__	186. Identify areas that need research.
✓	__	__	187. Review the literature on a research topic.
__	__	✓	188. Develop an appropriate research design.
__	✓	__	189. Apply a research experiment or method.
__	✓	__	190. Accurately report the results of research.
2	2	1	**Totals for this category.**

Now, go back through the 38 categories and find the ones where you had the most checks in the A columns. In the list of categories below, mark the ones in which you had five checks (or four checks if you did not have many fives and so on). Do a process of elimination to identify your top three categories.

Abilities Categories:

- ____ **Analysis/Conceptualizing**
- ____ **Problem Solving**
- ____ **Mechanical Repair**
- ____ **Artistic Expression**
- ____ **Musical Expression**
- ____ **Interpersonal Communication**
- ____ **Group Performance**
- ____ **Creative Writing**
- ____ **Technical Writing**
- ____ **Teaching/Training**
- ____ **Data Handling**
- ____ **Following Through**
- ____ **Detail Observation**
- ____ **Office Machine Operation**
- ____ **Financial Computing**
- ____ **Financial Management**
- ____ **Promoting**
- ____ **Negotiating**
- ____ **Selling**
- ____ **Independence/Self Management**
- ____ **Initiating Implementing**
- ____ **Creating/Innovating**
- ____ **Strategic Planning**
- ____ **Supervising/Managing**
- ____ **Leadership**
- ____ **Executive Leadership**
- ____ **Counseling/Coaching**
- ____ **Empathy Identification**
- ____ **Character Evaluation**
- ____ **Translating/Cultural Understanding**
- ____ **Cross-Cultural Relationships**
- ____ **Cross-Cultural Persuasion**
- ____ **Hand/Finger Coordination**
- ____ **Overall Coordination**
- ____ **Computer Skills**
- ____ **Cyber-Skills**
- ____ **Audio Video Production**
- ____ **Research**

My Top Three Abilities from the Narrative and Assessment

My top three abilities from the narrative section:

 # 1

 # 2

 # 3

My top three abilities from the abilities assessment:

1

2

3

Now may come the hardest part of all. Reduce everything to a final list of three in your own words.

At this point in my life, as best as I can tell, my top three abilities, the things I do the best, in their order of priority are:

1

2

3

Now transfer this final list of three to your PLM Worksheet. You have just completed two whole sections of your PLM worksheet.

You have completed the first section of your present wiring, which gave you a lot of detail about your personality.

You have completed the second section of your personal history, which covers the most important parts of your past that make you who you are.

More Than One in a Million

Do you realize that it is impossible for anyone to have the same PLM pieces you have filled in? Very few might have your present wiring, but nobody has your wiring and your history. Nobody.

This gives you a unique place in the world. But there are even greater things ahead as you look at the forces that are pulling you into the future. In the next and final section you will gain the final three pieces of your PLM design that will shape your Personal Life Mission.

We Saved the Best for Last

The final section is the most fun. It is the section where we begin dreaming about your future and the possibilities of your life. Get ready to consider what wonderful things your Designer might have had in mind when he laid out this unique individual called you.

Chapter 8

Discovering Your Interests:
Where You Will Apply Your Abilities

"I am looking for a lot of men who have an infinite capacity
to not know what can't be done."
Henry Ford

The Call of the Wild

About 100 years ago one of my favorite authors published his first great work.
I have worked on seal-hunting, sailing vessels off the coast of Japan in the 1900s. I have
joined the adventure of a gold rush in Alaska. I have experienced the life of an
exceptional dog taken from the suburbs of San Francisco and forced into service as a sled
dog in the Yukon. Jack London gave me all these experiences through his writings.

He is one of my favorites because of the content of his writing and because of the
intense dedication he showed to pursue his interests and reach his dream.

Jack London overcame a lack of education, a family so dysfunctional they would
make the Simpsons look like saints, and back-breaking poverty in a day and time when
there were no government social programs for the poor and no non-profit or church
charities available to him (Dyer, 1997).

Jack's father abandoned his mother when he heard she was pregnant with him.
His mother held séances and taught piano to make what she could. His stepfather was

gone frequently and their family moved from one rented place to another in the Oakland area about every three to six months because of their inability to pay the rent.

Jack left school after the eighth grade to help support himself and his family. From that point forward, for many years, Jack smoked constantly, abused alcohol, and worked in mind-numbing physical labor to survive. As a teenager he worked in canneries, as a farm laborer, and as an oyster-bed thief. For a time he hobo-ed across America, but found life difficult everywhere. At age 17 he signed on as a laborer on a seal-hunting ship bound for the Sea of Japan. On return he left with his brother-in-law to be part of the Klondike gold rush. He worked a claim for about a year without striking any big gold discoveries. However, he was gaining a different kind of gold he would trade in later.

After the Klondike he worked as a laundry-man for a hotel resort outside San Francisco. He worked ten and twelve hour days, six days a week, in a miserably hot environment washing and pressing linens. He would bicycle to and from work a long distance. He would be so tired when he got home all he could do was sleep until he had to get up for work the next day. A turning point came one day when he discovered that the resort was paying him one man's wages to do a job they had previously been paying two men to do. He quit and made a commitment to no longer sell himself as a beast of burden and to make a living with his mind, by writing.

Jack educated himself at the Oakland Library with the help of a gracious librarian who steered him in the direction of good books. He had an intense thirst for learning. Jack began writing short stories about his adventures at sea, in Alaska, and on the rails.

He submitted them to magazines. He was certain he had good stories to tell and could tell them well. He had entertained so many people before by telling of his adventures.

He continued to work odd jobs to keep some money coming in, but he poured himself into writing his stories and submitting them every waking hour that he did not have to work elsewhere. He went back and forth from being completely broke to having a little money. He pawned his typewriter and bicycle repeatedly through these ups and downs. He kept writing stories and submitting them and the rejection letters from editors began to stack up in his room.

Then a small break began to appear. Jack sold one of his articles for $75. He was ecstatic. He recovered all the things that were in pawn at the time. He continued to write but future acceptances were few and far between. But he kept at it.

His big break came in 1903 when a major magazine purchased his story, *The Call of the Wild*. From that point forward, Jack London skyrocketed to become the most famous and most successful American writer of his day. He would never again live in poverty or by demeaning and depressing labor.

I love his stories, *White Fang, The Sea Wolf, and The Story of Martin Eden*. I love the adventure and the art in his writing. I also love his personal story of overcoming adversity to follow a dream. He followed his interests and would not give up.

Your Interests Are Treasures of Distinction

Our world is full of areas of information and opportunity for pursuit from Aardvarks to Zulus. There are a million categories of things that can interest us. Each is like a magnet that will attract the attention of some people while not attracting others.

Some will attract you in a special way. They will capture your interest. And many more will be of no or little interest to you.

This is more than an academic exercise because your interests are treasures that distinguish you. Your interests will guide you from a life of boredom and mediocrity to a life of vitality and distinction.

Interests can be categories of knowledge or skills or experiences. We believe they are placed in you like hidden treasure. There is huge value in finding and trading in them.

Five Ways Your Interests Distinguish You

By *distinguish* we mean they set you apart as the special person you should be and they set you above the ordinary in what you achieve. Here are five ways your interests will distinguish you.

1. They focus your energies for success.

Peter Drucker (1991) said, "I am not sure there is a secret for success, but if there is one, it is the ability to focus. All persons and organizations, which succeed, are able to concentrate their efforts. Results come from concentrated effort."

Since there are a million things on which you can focus your mind and energies, there is a natural conspiracy against your success. The natural reaction to life is to move in a random pursuit from one thing to another. This produces failure because efforts are diffused.

Sometimes the most difficult task is not choosing where to focus, it is choosing not to focus on many other things that vie for our attention. Sometimes you have to say no to good things in order to say yes to better things. Identifying your interests clearly with priority will help you say no to an endless line of things that will demand your attention yet conspire against you.

"You can be anything you want." You have heard that saying and it is pretty true. You can't be a dolphin. But you can be a dolphin specialist in marine biology, if that is what you really want. If you really want to be a lawyer, you can be. If you want to be a professional pianist, you can be. So you can be anything you want, but you can't be everything. In other words, you have to choose. You can't be a marine biology/ dolphinologist lawyer professional pianist. You don't have the time. There is only one of you with one life.

After a great piano concert, a young man in the audience met the great pianist and said, "I'd give my life to be able to play like you." The pianist said, "I did."

As a young man, Luciano Pavorotti, one of the three tenors, couldn't decide whether he wanted to teach or wanted to sing. He thought that perhaps he could do both. His father wisely placed two chairs before him and told him to sit on both of them. Pavorotti ended up on the floor. His father told him that he couldn't sit in two chairs. He needed to focus his time and talents on one thing, to sit in one chair. The world is richer because of the choice he made.

Identifying your interests with clarity and priority will show what you should give your life to. It will distinguish you. The other option is to randomly piddle and have no distinction. You will spend your life on something, or you will waste it on nothing.

The interests you identify will direct you toward a Personal Life Mission that is worthy of your time, energies, and concentration. It will be worthy of your life.

2. They give you the courage to try.

The power of putting your interests in front of you on your PLM Worksheet is that they will give you the courage to try.

Jack London showed courage and commitment. He was clear in what he wanted.

3. They energize you to overcome obstacles.

Here's a promise. There will be obstacles to fulfilling your Personal Life Mission. Those who don't believe in you will criticize you. Small and threatened people who are jealous of you will put you down. Some will say you can't. Others will say you shouldn't. You will rely on people and they will let you down. Some will betray you. Some things will cost you money you don't have. Your own energy and health will fail you at some point. But if it is your Life Mission, and if you will not quit pursuing it, you will succeed.

This is where the interest stuff gets powerful. We're not just talking "interest" like it is just something that is mentally titillating. This is not just stuff you can walk away from. Your high priority "interests" map your destiny. Naming it, seeing it, and believing it give you the energy that is going to be required to overcome obstacles.

"If it were easy everyone would do it," another friend who owns his own insurance business said. He was talking about a challenge he has to bring his business into profitability. If he can, and he probably will, his potential for income is large. But he was right; many people will not do the difficult things. But those who do, have to have some kind of fuel that keeps them going.

Your top priority interests are the fuel that keeps you going when the going gets tough. If you quit and walk away from something for good, it was never one of your top interests. It was just a pastime.

That doesn't mean you won't have times of discouragement and even mental, physical, and spiritual exhaustion from trying to overcome obstacles. But it does mean that after you have rested, you will come back to it again. Your interests will fuel your engines for effort again and again.

4. They increase your personal capital.

We are not talking about financial capital, although that often follows. By personal capital we mean your value as one who can achieve good things. Any good thing counts, from a skill that is valued in the market place to the ability to counsel a person in crisis. Personal capital flows from what you know and what you can do. And these flow from the interests you have pursued.

Craig is a vice president of a brokerage firm that sells investments and precious metals. Part of his personal capital is his expertise as a numismatist, one who specializes in the history of and values of collectible coins. His expertise grew from his interest as a boy in collectible coins. He kept pursuing it to the level of being a specialist in the field who buys coins from around the world and sells them to major investors. He doesn't have a lot of personal capital as a plumber—that was not his interest and pursuit. There are, however, others who are interested in plumbing and in how to build a plumbing business, and they have a lot of personal capital.

We should be good stewards of our personal capital. Since God has given us opportunity to develop our knowledge and abilities to achieve good things, we should not squander it. We should be responsible. We should increase our personal capital as a matter of good stewardship. Too many view learning as a limited thing you do early in life to make it possible to make a living in some trade or profession. That is a low view of life and personal growth.

Being a life-long learner comes from a personal value that we are to increase our personal capital. We know all humans have basic worth. That is not what we are talking about. Only a few take building their personal capital seriously. But everyone should increase his or her knowledge and abilities as a lifestyle. It is financially beneficial and it is becoming even more necessary with the growing advances in technology. But even without that incentive, we should see ourselves as potential that should be developed, gold that should be mined.

We call the money that can be earned by loaning money "interest." This meaning comes from the same history of the meaning of "interest" as something that captures the mind. The consistent concept between the two different meanings is that there is benefit or profit in both kinds of interest. Financial interest adds profit to the capital invested. Mental interest motivates one to pursue something to gain value. The value is new knowledge and ability added to personal capital.

5. They compound your opportunities.

Simple interest, financially speaking, is value added to the principle amount. Compounded interest is value added to the principle amount plus some previously earned interest. Compounding interest can produce phenomenal returns.

You gain a simple benefit from pursuing your interests. You gain new knowledge and ability to achieve good things.

You also gain a compounded benefit from pursuing your interests. In their pursuit, you are exposed to brand new things in the world that can be new areas of pursuit: new people, new ideas, new places, and new opportunities. To compound our opportunities, we must identify our interests.

Identifying Your Interests

We will use two ways to identify interests, as we did with abilities in the last chapter. We will use a narrative approach with some general questions and an interest assessment.

Some Questions About Your Interests

"You are the people you meet and the books you read," a friend told me years ago. Now, twenty-five years later, I see how profoundly I have been shaped by my associations and reading. These two areas are also a way of identifying our interests.

Whom do you idolize? Who are your heroes? Who are the people whose stories fascinate you and make you wish you could live their experiences or have their abilities? You will usually choose people whose lives are full of the things in life that interest you.

I love the stories of adventurers who explored the oceans, Africa, the Amazon, Asia, and the Americas. I like to be around people who came up with strategies to make businesses or organizations succeed. I like to be around visionary people who saw opportunities and worked against obstacles to achieve their goals. Who are three of the most fascinating people to you, and what is it about their lives that interest you?

Fascinating People	What About Them Interests Me?
_____	_____
_____	_____
_____	_____

Now let's go to what you read. Your choice of reading material will reveal some of your interests. What have been the most enjoyable books? If you had a $100 gift certificate to the bookstore of your choice, what kind of book or books would you buy? Here is another one. A friend wants to buy you a subscription to any magazine you would like. What is the topic of the magazine? Or, you are going to the library and can check out a book, but you only have enough time to look at one section. What section will you choose? Write down your top three favorite topics for reading material.

Favorite Books or Magazines	Topics of Interest
_____	_____
_____	_____
_____	_____

Interest Assessment

This interest assessment is from the PathMaker™. It has 20 general categories of interest. There are 10 specific activities under each category. Go through each category and place a check (√) next to each activity in that category that interests you as something you might want to pursue. Before moving to the next category, add up the number of checks you made in that category and write that number in the "Totals for this category."

The Interest Assessment

Mechanical/Engineering

Designing, constructing, or repairing man-made objects from small intricate things like computer chips to large things like oil drilling platforms.

1. Repairing electrical appliances or machinery.
2. Building a house or a commercial building.
3. Drawing plans for construction.
4. Repairing automobile engines.
5. Working on a racing pit crew.
6. Drilling for oil or mining for minerals.
7. Building computers or electronics.
8. Designing weapons.
9. Building or repairing airplanes or boats.
10. Analyzing chemicals in a laboratory.

___ **Totals for this category.**

Machine Operations

Controlling, guiding, and/or driving machines.

11. Driving a tractor-trailer rig across the country.
12. Operating a bulldozer on a construction site.
13. Operating a ferry across a body of water.
14. Captaining a ship.
15. Driving a racecar.
16. Driving a delivery truck.
17. Driving bus.
18. Operating a forklift on a loading dock.
19. Conducting a train.
20. Flying airplanes.

___ **Totals for this category.**

Office/Clerical

Providing the support that enables an office to run smoothly and efficiently.

21. Scheduling appointments and meetings.
22. Keeping records and retrieving information.
23. Word processing on a computer.
24. Maintaining a filing system.
25. Greeting people in a busy office.
26. Making reports on needed information.
27. Entering data in a computer file system.
28. Packing and shipping supplies.
29. Organizing incoming and outgoing mail.
30. Receiving and directing incoming phone calls.

___ **Totals for this category.**

Physical Risk

Accomplishing tasks under dangerous or precarious conditions.

— 31. Leading a group on a mountain climbing expedition.
— 32. Keeping order in a potential riot situation.
— 33. Patrolling the outdoors as a game warden.
— 34. Investigating a burglary in progress.
— 35. Patrolling the border for illegal aliens.
— 36. Being a lifeguard at a beach.
— 37. Guiding a white-water trip.
— 38. Fighting in combat.
— 39. Fighting fires.
— 40. Policing a dangerous neighborhood.

— **Totals for this category.**

Helping Others

Meeting the needs of others in a tangible, hands-on manner.

— 41. Assisting visitors with their questions and concerns.
— 42. Organizing and catering a wedding or large function.
— 43. Direct parking lot traffic for a big event.
— 44. Serving guests at a big dinner.
— 45. Serving the needs of airline customers.
— 46. Setting up and breaking down equipment for a concert.
— 47. Cleaning offices or homes.
— 48. Caring for patients in a hospital
— 49. Giving physical therapy to injured patients.
— 50. Providing help for the elderly or disadvantaged.

— **Totals for this category.**

Writing

Using word-craft to communicate in an article, a book, a song, a poem, or a play.

— 51. Writing curriculum for education.
— 52. Writing music for a play or musical.
— 53. Writing news stories for a newspaper.
— 54. Selecting articles for publication in a magazine.
✓ 55. Writing a book or movie review.
— 56. Editing or proofreading a book.
— 57. Writing a script for a play or movie.
— 58. Writing narration for a video production.
— 59. Writing poetry or lyrics.
✓ 60. Writing books.

\ **Totals for this category.**

Artistic Expression

Expressing oneself creatively through tangible products or artistic medium.

_____ 61. Sculpting a statue or figure.
_____ 62. Designing architecture.
_____ 63. Decorating the interior of houses or buildings.
_____ 64. Designing landscape.
✓ 65. Photographing people or things.
_____ 66. Painting people, landscapes, or ideas.
_____ 67. Choreographing a dance routine.
_____ 68. Arranging flowers.
_____ 69. Drawing illustrations.
_____ 70. Designing clothing.

1 **Totals for this category.**

Finance

Planning financial strategies and managing money.

_____ 71. Keeping financial records.
_____ 72. Preparing budgets for large organizations.
_____ 73. Analyzing and recommending investments.
_____ 74. Doing accounting and bookkeeping.
_____ 75. Managing the financial office of an organization.
_____ 76. Providing insurance for individuals or businesses.
_____ 77. Working as a bank teller.
_____ 78. Evaluating loan applications.
_____ 79. Processing mortgages and loans.
_____ 80. Preparing taxes and giving tax advice.

_____ **Totals for this category.**

Performing

Expressing oneself to an audience or taking part in a creative performance.

_____ 81. Hosting a radio or television show.
_____ 82. Putting on a magic show.
_____ 83. Being a radio or television news reporter or anchor.
_____ 84. Narrating a play.
_____ 85. Presenting a speech.
_____ 86. Acting in a play or theater.
_____ 87. Reading poetry.
_____ 88. Serving as a master of ceremonies.
_____ 89. Doing stand-up comedy.
_____ 90. Acting in a movie or television show.

_____ **Totals for this category.**

Persuasion

Using strong verbal skills and your personality to convince others to support a product, service, idea, or person.

__	91. Arguing a legal case in court.
__	92. Preparing an advertising campaign.
__	93. Lobbying members of Congress.
__	94. Selling real estate, insurance, or financial services.
__	95. Managing the sales department for a company.
__	96. Being a public relations officer for a company.
__	97. Working in or managing a political campaign.
__	98. Persuading a company to agree to a large contract.
__	99. Promoting concerts or being a personal agent.
__	100. Debating philosophical, political, or religious ideas.

__ **Totals for this category.**

Teaching/Instructing

Helping people learn a new skill or information or to deepen their understanding or expertise.

__	101. Teaching at a college or university.
__	102. Teaching at a junior high or high school.
__	103. Teaching at a grade school.
__	104. Teaching preschool.
__	105. Teaching special education.
✓	106. Teaching adults in a business setting.
__	107. Leading corporate training seminars.
__	108. Teaching physical education, sports or outdoor recreation
✓	109. Teaching religious studies in a group, church, or school.
✓	110. Tutoring students.

3 **Totals for this category.**

Leadership/Management

Acquiring and maintaining followers and/or giving supervision to people in an organization.

✓	111. Envisioning new directions that need to be pursued.
✓	112. Inspiring others to pursue a direction with you.
✓	113. Empowering others to use their abilities.
✓	114. Modeling character and excellence to others.
✓	115. Encouraging those who follow you.
✓	116. Being responsible for the outputs of subordinates.
✓	117. Selecting capable people.
__	118. Assigning the right work.
__	119. Appraising subordinate effectiveness.
__	120. Initiating removal of incompetent subordinates.

7 **Totals for this category.**

Plants and Animals

Working with plants and animals to understand, grow, nurture, train, preserve, heal, or control them.

___ 121. Helping ranchers improve their livestock.
___ 122. Doing marine research or management.
___ 123. Being a veterinarian or a caretaker.
___ 124. Training animals.
___ 125. Doing animal research or preservation.
___ 126. Being a forester or farmer or rancher.
___ 127. Teaching better farming and ranching in poor countries.
___ 128. Building or managing landscapes.
___ 129. Working in a greenhouse or nursery.
___ 130. Researching methods of greater food production.

___ **Totals for this category.**

Cross-Cultural Communication

Interacting with and understanding people of other cultures.

___ 131. Learning a new language.
___ 132. Living with people in a foreign country.
___ 133. Researching different cultures.
___ 134. Teaching foreigners the culture of your country.
___ 135. Meeting and building relationships with internationals.
___ 136. Serving as an ambassador to a foreign nation.
___ 137. Translating.
___ 138. Teaching English as a second language abroad.
___ 139. Working for the government or a company abroad.
___ 140. Serving as a foreign missionary or with the Peace Corps.

___ **Totals for this category.**

Meeting Physical Needs

Meeting and caring for the physical needs of people.

___ 141. Being a physical therapist.
___ 142. Being a doctor.
___ 143. Providing services for the blind, deaf, or mute.
___ 144. Providing services for the elderly.
___ 145. Meeting the needs of the poor.
___ 146. Working in or managing a rescue mission.
___ 147. Building Habitat for Humanity homes.
___ 148. Working in the Special Olympics.
___ 149. Being a dentist or orthodontist.
___ 150. Being a nurse.

___ **Totals for this category.**

Counseling

Helping people come to terms with their lives and make positive decisions and behavioral changes.

_____ 151. Helping people deal with emotional issues.
_____ 152. Helping married couples save their marriages.
_____ 153. Helping parents and children in conflicts.
_____ 154. Counseling children with emotional problems.
_____ 155. Counseling people with grief or post-traumatic stress.
_____ 156. Providing educational and career counseling.
✓ 157. Providing pastoral or spiritual counseling.
_____ 158. Doing one-on-one clinical counseling.
_____ 159. Leading group therapy.
✓ 160. Teaching counseling truths to an audience.

2 **Totals for this category.**

Musical Expression

Expressing oneself through instruments, lyrics, singing, arranging, or dance.

_____ 161. Playing an instrument.
_____ 162. Writing lyrics.
_____ 163. Composing and/or arranging music.
_____ 164. Singing.
_____ 165. Dancing.
_____ 166. Choreographing.
_____ 167. Conducting an orchestra or leading a band.
_____ 168. Producing and/or recording.
_____ 169. Leading a choir or vocal group.
_____ 170. Producing a musical show.

_____ **Totals for this category.**

Motivational Leadership

Leading people to accomplish personal or organizational goals.

✓ 171. Leading the expansion of an organization.
✓ 172. Leading the beginning of new organization.
_____ 173. Leading the turn-around of a failing organization.
_____ 174. Motivating people to excel in education.
_____ 175. Raising money for a good cause.
_____ 176. Raising volunteer support for a good cause.
_____ 177. Organizing to get a big project accomplished.
✓ 178. Inspiring followers through speaking.
✓ 179. Inspiring followers through your behavior.
✓ 180. Being a motivational speaker.

5 **Totals for this category.**

Facility Administration

Managing a campus, buildings, and/or grounds.

___ 181. Choosing the best site for a new building.
___ 182. Managing a maintenance and security staff.
___ 183. Managing traffic and security for a large campus.
___ 184. Scheduling the use of a large facility.
___ 185. Managing a sports arena.
___ 186. Managing the budget for maintenance, utilities, new construction and security for a large facility.
___ 187. Managing large landscaping and grounds.
___ 188. Purchasing supplies and equipment.
___ 189. Golf course or resort facility management.
___ 190. Managing janitorial services for a large facility.

___ **Totals for this category.**

Research

Obtaining information by observation, study, experiments, or interviews and analyzing it statistically or qualitatively.

___ 191. Designing a process for collecting information.
___ 192. Reviewing the literature on a research topic.
___ 193. Identifying areas that need research.
___ 194. Apply a research experiment on people or things.
___ 195. Report and publish the results of research.
___ 196. Evaluating statistical information.
___ 197. Observing people, animals, or things.
___ 198. Testing people to form a database of information.
___ 199. Interviewing people.
___ 200. Supervising research projects.

___ **Totals for this category.**

Based on your responses to the Interest Assessment, rank your top four interest categories below. First transfer the "Totals for this category" to each category below, and then rank your top three categories in their order of priority.

___ **Mechanical/Engineering**
___ **Machine Operations**
___ **Office and Clerical**
___ **Physical Risk**
___ **Helping Others**
___ **Writing**
___ **Artistic Expression**
___ **Finance**
___ **Performing**

- **Persuasion**
- **Teaching and Instruction**
- **Leadership/ Management**
- **Plants and Animals**
- **Cross-Cultural Communication**
- **Meeting Physical Needs**
- **Counseling**
- **Musical Expression**
- **Motivational Leadership**
- **Facility Administration**
- **Research**

My top three categories of interest from the Interest Assessment are:

1. _____ HELPING OTHERS

2. _____ WRITING

3. _____ COUNSELLING

Considering your interests from this assessment *and* the people you find interesting, *and* the reading you find interesting, what are your top three interests?

My Top Three Interests

1. INVESTMENTS _____

2. MENTORING _____

3. LEADERSHIP _____

Now transfer these top three interests to your "Interests" box on your PLM Worksheet.

The Power Connection Between Abilities and Interests

There is an important power connection between abilities and interests. Abilities are like an electrical outlet—there is power waiting there to be applied to something. Interests are the appliances or tools that you plug into the power found in abilities.

So if you have the ability of promoting and the interest of artistic expression, your power connection might be selling art, promoting an artist, selling your own art, or being a concert promoter.

Jack London's interests were in the adventures of the western outdoors. His abilities were in telling stories with his pen. When he plugged his interests into his abilities, the result was powerful.

Interests   **Abilities**

Take some time to ponder what power connections you might have between your abilities and your interests. There is probably some hidden treasure there.

You have only two more boxes to go on the PLM Worksheet! You have done a lot and it will reward you a lot, too. Keep up the good work. The next two boxes are extremely important. In fact, for many people they are the missing pieces to discovering their Personal Life Missions. In the next two chapters, you will discover what kind of results your work must have in order for you to keep going. After all, you may have the electrical outlet (abilities) and the tools (interests), but if you aren't motivated to plug it in, it won't do any good!

Chapter 9

Discovering Your Essential Outcomes:
Sustained Motivation

"Eighty percent of success is showing up."
Woody Allen

"Destiny is not a matter of chance; it is a matter of choice.
It is not a thing to be waited for; it is a thing to be achieved."
William Jennings Bryan

"It has always been my ambition to preach the gospel
where Christ was not known…"
The Apostle Paul
(Romans 15:20 NIV)

Hell Was in a UPS Truck

No offense to UPS. In fact I appreciate them hiring me at a time when I

desperately needed a job with benefits for my family. But one of my dark hours came one

evening while I was loading boxes in a UPS semi-tractor trailer in Denver.

I was at a point in my life of transition. I left one job in abject frustration because

I was forced into a mold that was the opposite of my wiring. It left me emotionally,

physically, and spiritually wiped out. To move in the direction I thought I needed to go, I

had to continue my education toward a graduate degree. I had to work some "have to"

jobs in order to get my education and get to my "want to" job. My wife and I had two

little kids and were expecting a third. And life sucked.

It was winter and bone cold. It was one of my "off" days from school. That meant

I worked the day hours in construction and after dinner went to my UPS shift. I sat on the frozen parking lot of UPS, which I affectionately called "The Big House," for a few more minutes in my heated truck before I absolutely had to go in.

That night we got hammered. The boxes were coming down the line to us in our trucks like a stampede. We loaders had to read the label codes on each of the boxes to be sure they were supposed to be in our trucks, then build walls with them from the front to the back as quickly as we could. Although I wasn't too good at reading and catching mis-loads, building the walls was an art at which I possessed some acumen. And I was building them like a madman.

One of the foam insulation cushions on the dock that my tractor-trailer was backed up to was missing so cold air and blowing snow kept swirling in my truck. Although you could have hung meat in there, I wasn't cold. Loaders always break a sweat keeping up with the flow on a night like that.

In those days, working hard physically was not uncommon for me. I kind of liked it. But that night I reached a point of breaking. I didn't break physically but emotionally.

As I was loading, I became angry. Then I became angrier. Then I quit reading the labels on the boxes. Then I quit handling the boxes with proper UPS care and quit building proper UPS walls. I started chucking them harder and harder in heaps. Then I began to cry and cuss and cry and cuss. Finally, I cried and prayed, "God, why have you forsaken me in this rotten, stinking, worthless place! This is not what I was created for!"

That night as I walked out of the Big House, I gave my supervisor my two weeks notice. I resolved to move heaven and hell and do just about anything else to replace the benefits I was getting there, but I would not continue to work there anymore. The machine-like work was mind numbing and spirit depressing to me.

My Number One Essential Outcome Is Influencing People

You see, my number one Essential Outcome is influencing people. I live to have an impact on other people for the better. Without it I am nothing. My construction job was not a lot better, but at least it gave me some contact with customers who would enjoy what I was building for them. But loading those stinking boxes in a truck gave me absolutely no sense of having positive influence and impact on peoples' lives. I reasoned any moron (that's harsh, I know, but I had had it) could do what I was doing. But it was not why I was created.

I thank God that today I have the opportunity to work in a job where I can influence people for the better. In fact, I hope to even impact you for the better through this PLM process. And I love it. It is my number one Essential Outcome.

Definition of Essential Outcomes

When we use Essential Outcomes in this eighth PLM box, what we mean is this: Essential Outcomes are the basic characteristics or results that an activity must have in order for you to apply yourself fully for an extended time. For short we will call them EOs.

At first, I was pretty motivated at UPS because it was kind of fun and motivating to learn their system and rise to the challenge. And the benefits were good. But in time I not only lost motivation, I was demoralized.

Let's look at the key components of our definition of EOs. First, they are the basic characteristics or results of activities. In other words, every job, chore, hobby, or pursuit has certain characteristics and results. There are qualities and outcomes that are part of every activity.

Second, your EOs keep you motivated to apply yourself fully. We all know the difference between half-hearted efforts and really applying ourselves. When a job or task is full of our EOs, we find motivation from within to apply ourselves fully.

I like motivational speakers and books. I have benefited from them. But some people have to keep pumping themselves up with motivational materials because their jobs are devoid of their Essential Outcomes. They are demoralized because they are doing the wrong things. That's my beef with some multi-level marketing programs. They suck people into work by the incentive of greed for better things and guilt for not being more successful than they are. Then they keep them pumped with motivational speakers and materials to get them up for one more round of leaning on their friends to buy stuff they don't want and to do things they don't want to do.

Finally, EOs sustain motivation. Almost anyone can do most jobs or activities for a little while, but to pursue something completely over a long period of time and maintain sanity, it has to be full of your EOs.

EO's Are the Essence of What You Must Experience

There is a Latin phrase that relates to the words "essence" and "essentials." It is *sine qua non*. It means, "Without, there is none." Your Essentials are the characteristics an activity has to have for you to experience the essence of who you are. When you are forced to focus most of your energies on things that do not possess your EOs, you begin to cease to exist mentally. You feel like you don't exist. Without it, you feel like nothing. The result will first be anger. Then it will turn to depression, then to despair.

However, when your job or hobby is full of one or more of your EOs, you feel complete and motivated and optimistic.

Steve and I periodically consult people whose lives and careers allow them to fulfill most of the nine PLM boxes except this one, and they are miserable. Often they make great money and have advanced in great careers, but they are sick of it. They are frustrated because they don't know why they are sick of it. They aren't finding their EOs.

Discovering Your Essential Outcomes

The following list contains thirty Essential Outcomes. To discover your top three, read through the list and the descriptions of each one and respond to them. Check off the response after each EO and its description that best reflects how you feel. Remember, these can be the characteristics and/or results of many activities you might do.

Being In Control

You value being in charge. You want to be the one who decides what to do and when to do it. You like to direct the action and be in a position to determine what others should do in a project. You like being the leader.

_____ I definitely need this   ✓ I prefer this   _____ I don't care

Designing and Creating

You value being able to invent or design things. You want freedom to do things your way. You like being able to pursue the many ideas you have. You prefer to start from nothing than with someone else's idea.

_____ I definitely need this   __✓_ I prefer this   _____ I don't care

Developing Potential

You see potential in people or things. You want to develop the potential you see.

_____ I definitely need this   __✓_ I prefer this   _____ I don't care

Physical Exertion

You want the chance to get out and get active. You enjoy the feeling of strenuous activity. Being sedentary at a desk job drives you crazy.

_____ I definitely need this   __✓_ I prefer this   _____ I don't care

Accuracy and Perfection

You value doing things right and people who don't irritate you. You like paying attention to the details. You like to have your name on things that are done right.

_____ I definitely need this   __✓_ I prefer this   _____ I don't care

Being Persuasive

You like convincing others of the value of an idea, concept, or product. You like persuading others by communication or by your relationship with them.

_____ I definitely need this   _✓_ I prefer this   _____ I don't care

Meeting Needs and Fulfilling Expectations

You enjoy being of service. You enjoy feeling the appreciation of others for your services. You like to know what needs to be done for success and doing it.

_✓_ I definitely need this   _____ I prefer this   _____ I don't care

Mobility

You like being on the move. You dislike being stuck in one place or environment for too long. You at least need windows but at most need to get around to different locations to do your work or activities.

_____ I definitely need this   _____ I prefer this   _✓_ I don't care

Supervising Others

You like to manage others and have a desire to oversee and motivate others to meet objectives.

_____ I definitely need this   _____ I prefer this   _✓_ I don't care

Influencing Others

You want to influence how others think and impact how they live. You want to make a difference in peoples' lives and help shape them so they are better off because of your part in their lives.

    __✓__ I definitely need this   ____ I prefer this   ____ I don't care

Creativity

You want to come up with new things and ideas. You like an environment that fosters creative freedom and expression. You like being the first to come up with things. If it is fresh and new and smart, you like it.

    ____ I definitely need this   ____ I prefer this   __✓__ I don't care

Risk

You like risk. You feel emotionally and physically energized by taking a risk in order to experience or achieve something extraordinary.

    ____ I definitely need this   __✓__ I prefer this   ____ I don't care

Challenge

You are motivated by challenges that stretch you and make you rise to new levels of achievement. You enjoy taking on things that many others fear to do.

    __✓__ I definitely need this   ____ I prefer this   ____ I don't care

Troubleshooting

You like to go into situations where there are problems or breakdowns in the system, equipment or organization and analyze it, diagnose the problem, and fix it.

_____ I definitely need this _____ I prefer this __✓_ I don't care

Autonomy and Independence

You want freedom and independence. You want to work without supervision. You want to set your own schedule and agenda.

_____ I definitely need this __✓_ I prefer this _____ I don't care

Competition

You like to compete against others for financial and recognition rewards. It energizes you and you have confidence you can win. And you like winning.

_____ I definitely need this _____ I prefer this __✓_ I don't care

Problem Solving

You like going into places with difficult problems, because you like solving them. You like to overcome obstacles to find solutions. If there are not problems to solve, you go looking for them. When there are no problems for you to solve, life gets boring.

_____ I definitely need this __✓ I prefer this _____ I don't care

Teaching

You like to teach others new knowledge and skills. You enjoy the growth you see in those you teach.

_____ I definitely need this   ✓ I prefer this   _____ I don't care

Structured Organization

You want things structured and organized. You want things to happen as they should and when they should. You need to know what is expected of you. You need consistency in your environment and experiences.

_____ I definitely need this   _____ I prefer this   ✓ I don't care

Goal Achievement

You like to achieve clear objectives. You want to see them clearly in front of you, work on them, and enjoy the closure when you achieve them.

✓ I definitely need this   _____ I prefer this   _____ I don't care

Exploration

You want to explore new things in life. You want to move past what has already been discovered and charted to new places, ideas, and experiences.

✓ I definitely need this   _____ I prefer this   _____ I don't care

Recognition

You like to be appreciated and recognized for your contributions to life. You want others to be aware of what you have accomplished and to honor you for it.

_____ I definitely need this   √ I prefer this   _____ I don't care

Competency

You want to master your work and be an expert in it. You strive for excellence and the highest levels of proficiency.

_____ I definitely need this   √ I prefer this   _____ I don't care

Affirmation

You want to know that you are doing a good job. If you are not doing a good job, you want to know so you can adjust so you can do a good job.

_____ I definitely need this   √ I prefer this   _____ I don't care

Identity

You want to see how your task fits into the bigger picture of what is being done so you feel you are contributing to something worthwhile.

_____ I definitely need this   √ I prefer this   _____ I don't care

Analysis

You like to research and analyze information to form conclusions and solutions. You like to sift through a lot of information that can lead you to understanding.

_____ I definitely need this   __✓_ I prefer this   _____ I don't care

Strategy

You like to look at physical or mental problems and think through ways to solve them. You like to think through the moves and countermoves in order to make a smart move. You like to consider the odds.

_____ I definitely need this   __✓ I prefer this   _____ I don't care

Adventure

You like to take on adventures that combine some risk and exploration and challenge to experience the thrill of having strived valiantly to achieve greatly.

_____ I definitely need this   __✓ I prefer this   _____ I don't care

Security

You like to have your life ordered to avoid all unnecessary risks. You want to be safe in all areas, from finances to job security to physical safety.

_____ I definitely need this   _____ I prefer this   __✓ I don't care

Beauty

You love to create and experience beauty. You value beauty as a key component of life that makes it worthwhile. You want to beautify the world for yourself and others through your art, craft or work.

_____ I definitely need this   _____ I prefer this   _√_ I don't care

Now Let's Prioritize Your EOs

Now, look back through your responses and transfer checks from the EOs that you checked "I definitely need this" to the list below.

_____ Being in Control

_____ Designing and Creating

_____ Developing Potential

_____ Physical Exertion

_____ Accuracy and Perfection

_____ Being Persuasive

✳ _√_ Meetings Needs and Fulfilling Expectations

_____ Mobility

_____ Supervising Others

✳ _√_ Influencing Others

_____ Creativity

_____ Risk

✳ _√_ Challenge

_____ Troubleshooting

_____ Autonomy and Independence

_____ Competition

_____ Problem Solving

_____ Teaching

_____ Structured Organization

__✓__ Goal Achievement

__✓__ Exploration

_____ Recognition

_____ Competency

_____ Affirmation

_____ Identity

_____ Analysis

_____ Strategy

_____ Adventure

_____ Security

_____ Beauty

From the checked EOs in the list, make a short list of the three you have to have in any activity or job or pursuit to keep doing it long-term.

If you had to take a job and knew it had to last a long time and could only have one of these EOs in it, which would you choose? Write #1 next to it. Then write #2 and #3 next to the others in their order of priority for you.

Transfer your top three EOs to your PLM Worksheet (Appendix A). Congratulations on identifying your EOs. By identifying your Essential Outcomes, you have gained something that very few people in the world have. You have gained an understanding of what kinds of things you must be doing to sustain motivation. While others are losing heart for their pursuits, you will become better at choosing the kinds of jobs and activities that move you to keep giving your best.

We live in a competitive world. And to be great at anything, we have to apply ourselves over time. So to compete in the job market or the marketplace of businesses, or to have something extraordinary to give the world, we better know what we are going to want to do for a long time. We need to know what will sustain our motivation.

By now you are seeing what it is about your job and other pursuits that either energizes you or leaves you flat. We are getting closer to our final chapters of applying what you are learning about your PLM pieces to your life. But first, we have the final PLM piece. It is the most important piece of all.

If interests are in our heads, and if our Essential Outcomes come from our hearts, the next piece, Passion, comes from our guts. Let's go to chapter ten and identify your passion.

Chapter 10

Discovering Your Passion:
The Most Important Piece of All

"Jesus ... who for the joy set before him endured the cross ..."
Hebrews 12:2

"One can never consent to creep when one feels an impulse to soar."
Helen Keller

"Success is not the result of spontaneous combustion. You must set yourself on fire."
Reggie Leach

"Personally summoned by the Creator of the universe, we are given a meaning in what we do that flames over every second and inch of our lives. Challenged, inspired, rebuked, and encouraged by God's call, we cannot for a moment settle down to the comfortable, the mediocre, the banal, and the boring."
Os Guinness, *The Call*

The Dream

In 1954 a lady caught the bus on the way home from work. She was bone tired. After she was seated, a man told her to move to the back of the bus so he could have her seat. She refused.

The police were called to arrest Rosa Parks for refusing to give up her seat to a white man. Then a phone call went out to a local pastor whom God had been preparing for a great Personal Life Mission that has blessed the world.

Dr. Martin Luther King, Jr. had a passion that God had been stirring within him. As a young man he told one of his friends that someday he was going to be a great man.

He went to Morehouse College where he graduated in 1948. He was ordained a Baptist minister that same year. He then attended and graduated from Crozer Theological Seminary. Finally, he received his Ph.D. from Boston University (Warner, 1999).

God was preparing Dr. King for his mission. He was gaining knowledge, wisdom, and skill. He was wrestling with the biggest social issues of his day. He studied the works of Paul Tillich, a German theologian who fled Nazi Germany in 1933. Tillich was concerned with racial peace and how Christianity must address it. He saw the evils of racism firsthand in Nazi Germany. His views helped Dr. King form his own.

Upon graduation from seminary, Dr. King could have gone to work with his father in the prestigious Ebenezer Baptist Church in Atlanta, Georgia. Some found it interesting that he accepted a pastorate at the more obscure Dexter Avenue Baptist Church in Montgomery, Alabama. Some wondered why Dr. King was not taking a stronger career move in a stronger location to deal with issues of racism. But God knew. He had his person in the right place at the right time.

Dr. King took the call about Rosa Park's arrest. That phone call ignited his calling from God. It exposed the fire of his passion. It propelled him into the Civil Rights Movement with him leading the 1955-56 boycott of the Montgomery city busses.

He began to give sermons and talks around the country on civil rights and he co-founded the Southern Christian Leadership Conference in 1957 for the purpose of working for civil rights (Warner, 1999).

He moved with the SCLC to Atlanta in 1960 where he became co-pastor of the Ebenezer Church with his father. King led demonstrations throughout the south with his greatest day being the march on Washington on August 28, 1963 where he delivered his famous eight-minute "I have a dream" message (Warner, 1999). He was awarded the Nobel Peace Prize in 1964. On April 3, 1968 at the Masonic Temple in Memphis, Tennessee, King delivered his "I've been to the mountain top" message in support of the Memphis sanitation workers' strike for better wages and conditions. The following day he was shot to death while standing on a balcony of his motel.

Dr. King galvanized the Civil Rights Movement and was its most effective leader. The Voting Rights Act of 1966 was passed because of his leadership. He is revered today as one of the greatest leaders for justice and equality. He is respected for his commitment to nonviolent protest. He believed in nonviolent action by the examples of Jesus and Mahatma Gandhi (Gardner, 1995).

We all want to live in a society where people "Are not judged by the color of their skin, but by the content of their character." We are a little closer to that reality today because a man embraced his passion from God.

Passion Is Not Pleasure, It Is Pain

Passion is not the pleasure of romance. It is the pain we carry in our hearts of something we must do because it ought to be done.

The word "passion" goes back to the 1200s, and until the 1600s it was used exclusively for the affliction of Jesus Christ when he was crucified (Barnhardt, 1988). That gives some great insight. Jesus Christ had a passion to do something that had to be done even though it was painful. Passion really can be a cross in that it may be the hardest thing in our lives we will do, but it will produce the greatest results of anything we do.

When we do use "passion" in a romantic way, it means we love someone so much it hurts. There may be something you must do with your life that you must do so badly it hurts. It is your cross. It is your affliction of the heart.

Why Do We Have Passion?

Passion is exclusive to humans. My dogs have no aspirations to change the world or impact the canine kingdom. They just want to eat, sleep, be petted, and go chase ducks at the lake.

Passion comes from a great human conflict. We are made in the image of God, yet we live in a world that is damaged by evil. Do you see the problem?

We have an inborn sense of right, justice, honor, morality, and purpose. But we live in a world where evil tries to produce wrong, injustice, disgrace, immorality, and chaos. So our lives are a quest to rise above what makes our souls ache and help others do the same. We can't just be content to eat, sleep, be petted, and go chase ducks at the lake. Some people have lost their passion and just go through the motions. Paul Simon said, "We're working our jobs, collect our pay. We think we're gliding down the highway, when in fact we're slip-slidin' away." We are meant to be passionate people. We are in a spiritual battle for the very aspirations of our souls.

One person may engage the battle as a movie producer whose films shape the values of our culture. Another may engage the battle as a researcher seeking a cure for cancer. And another may engage it as a potato chip delivery person who volunteers to build houses with Habitat for Humanity.

Passion is part of the human experience. Some may have it more than others, but most of us know what it means to have a soul-ache about something that needs to be corrected.

Passion Will Never Die

Your passion will never die. It will try to come out in one way or another in all your significant endeavors. Some have a passion that has not been verbalized or expressed in a clear way. It motivates and directs, but it does so in a covert way.

Seeing and naming your passion can help you overtly manage your life to fulfill it. It will be the core thread in your Personal Life Mission.

What is the pain you carry in your heart over something you must do because it ought to be done?

Where to Look for Your Passion

1. Look at your story. You are a story. We believe in providence, meaning that God has been the one writing your story for a reason. Just as Dr. King had a story that shaped his passion, so do you. As you consider all the pieces on your PLM Worksheet, what is your story?

2. Look at the ordinary. You acquire your passion from very normal life experiences. Only a very few people have a passion from some kind of mystical or spiritual lightning experience. Don't look for angels or burning bushes. Look for everyday people kinds of experiences.

3. Look at your emotions. Even though your passion probably does not come from a lightning experience, it does produce thunder in your heart. It pushes your buttons. It can move you to tears, anger, or rapture. Passion is emotional by definition.

4. Look at your fears. The fear comes from the risks you will have to take to pursue your passion. You are going to have to risk failure, ridicule, and potential loss to fulfill your passion. That is why we believe God gives us the emotional passion to do it. God knows we have to have an incredible motivation right from the middle of our guts to move against our fears, which are also in the middle of our guts, to accomplish great things.

Three Q's and A's to Discover Your Passion

There are three questions and answers that will help you discover the pain in your heart over something you must do because it ought to be done.

1. What moves me?

I was glad that none of my family was in the living room the night I watched Kari Strug of the U.S. Women's Gymnastic Olympic Team make her historical vault at the summer games in Barcelona, Spain. She had sprained her ankle on her previous attempt, and she had one more vault to go. The scoring was tight. It was not clear if the U.S. Women's Team would take the gold without a high score from her. But one thing was clear: her career and destiny would be shaped by this one challenge.

She choked back the tears from the pain in her ankle. Her coach, Bela Kuroli, preached words of encouragement to her. "You can do it! I know you can do it!" She

166

stood at the starting line and bit her lip in concentration. She sprinted to the vault, made her leap, came down on a perfect landing, then quickly raised her weight off her ankle in pain as she smiled from ear to ear to the wild screams of the crowd.

I cried like a baby. I sat there on my sofa, an emotional mess, watching this 85-pound pixie show enormous guts.

People who strive against obstacles to do great things always move me. The greater the obstacles and the striving, the more emotions thunder within me.

My wife has a different passion. She is moved by the injustice of people who are mistreated. Her anger and defensiveness well up every time she senses injustice. The mortal sin our children can commit in front of her is to degrade someone else by calling them a name or mistreating them. I think she got it from her dad. One of the few times I saw him red with anger was when a person in power was abusing a subordinate.

What moves you? What kinds of events or experiences bring up tears, anger, or sheer joy? What brings a thunder of emotion in your heart every time? That may be a clue to your passion. Take a minute and journal some of your thoughts. What moves you?

_____

_____

_____

2. What do you hate?

Your mother may have taught you that you are not to say you hate anything. You dislike things, but you do not hate them.

With all due respect to our mothers, we do hate some things. If you can only plug in one thing, how would you complete this sentence? "I hate _____

_____."

You have several answers, but there is probably one that stands out above all the rest. I have several answers myself, but I also have one that stands out above the rest. I hate it when people waste their lives. That drives me nuts. It seems to me to be the ultimate irresponsible squandering of the ultimate resource and opportunity.

I get angry over a man who is wasting his life as a drug addict, or someone wasting his life as a multi-millionaire who lives simply to make another deal and another dollar. Life is more than sensory titillation. The drug addict titillates his senses with narcotics to the loss of family, friends, and a positive impact on others. A money addict titillates his senses with the thrill of making more money often to the loss of family, friends, and a positive impact on others. It is really living with no more purpose than my dogs. And I hate that.

That is why I aspire to live with higher purpose, and why I live to help others do the same. In the blank part of the sentence above, write in the number one thing you hate.

3. If God would let me accomplish anything in the world, what would I choose?

This is the ultimate dream question. Some may ask it by saying if money were no object at all, if you possessed enough wealth to do anything and you could not fail, what would you do? So many of us are so preoccupied with dreaming about wealth itself and winning the lottery, we don't really even think about what we would want to do with it. You can only eat so much food, take so many trips, and wear so many clothes. What do you do beyond titillating your senses? If you could accomplish anything with your life, what would you choose?

If you are at a loss, welcome to the club. Most of us have to spend so much energy on just making a living that we rarely if ever think on this level. But doing so can help you uncover your true passions. And even though you will never have all the money in the world, you can begin to line up your life to pursue your passion.

Journal your thoughts. What would you do if God would let you do anything, or if money were no object. Try to list things beyond the titillating things you would do at first to just have fun, like buying a Porsche.

_____

_____

_____

Now transfer your answers to your PLM worksheet.

From a Bad Student to a Published Author

Kathy Peel (Peel, 1997) sat in a motivational seminar her husband, Bill, was leading for a group of couples. One session was on pursuing your dreams. She had heard it before, but thought, "Yeah, that stuff is good for others but I am a busy mom with three boys and a husband to raise." Bill challenged everyone to take some time to write down what in their heart of hearts they would like to do.

She did that and was surprised at her answer. It was, "Write a book."

It was surprising because she had not made stellar grades in school. And her friends knew she did not get stellar grades in school. So it seemed to be a weird desire. What did she think she was doing? But it was her true desire flowing from a passion.

She began writing about a topic she knew well and does with excellence: family management. Over the years, Kathy had collected all kinds of tips from all kinds of sources on family management, and she had some tricks of her own. She really approached family management as a job.

She talked her husband into agreeing to publishing the book themselves. They put up the money, had it printed, and she went on the campaign trail to bookstores and every thinkable venue to sell her book. She hoped for several thousand sales. A Mother's Manual for Summer Survival has sold 350,000 copies. It launched her into a new career as a writer, speaker, and consultant.

Kathy is now the founder of The Family Manager, she serves on the staff of *Family Circle* magazine, and has written twelve books, including *The Family Manager* and *Do Plastic Surgeons Take Visa*?

I just saw Kathy Peel the other day on a television magazine show. She was giving tips to women on how to get the male members of the household to help with housework. And she was good. It reminded me of what happens when people pursue their passion.

Kathy pursued her passion and is helping many others.

Congratulations! You have completed all nine pieces of your unique design.

You have just put together the pieces that will form your Personal Life Mission. Right now they may look like disjointed pieces that do not all fit or make sense together.

You are going to experience an exciting thing. As you go to the next chapter, you will begin seeing the pieces take shape into a direction, and you will write the first draft of your PLM statement.

Even more exciting is going to be your life experience from now on. We predict that every year you are going to experience two things. First, you will understand each piece better. Second, you will see the pieces continue to line up for an overall purpose in your life. You will experience the joy of finding your place in the world and being all you can be in that fit.

Now let's go from your PLM pieces to your actual Personal Life Mission Statement. This is going to be powerful in your life.

Chapter 11

Choosing the Stone for Your Sculpture:
Writing Your First PLM Statement

"When you know your dream, know that you are worthy of that dream."
John-Roger and Peter McWilliams

"He is a wise man who wastes no energy on the pursuits for which he is not fitted;
and he is still wiser who, from the things he can do well,
chooses and resolutely follows the best."
William Gladstone

Choosing the Stone for Your Sculpture

Have you ever watched someone sculpt a statue? First, the sculptor can see the finished project in mind. Knowing that, the sculptor selects the stone. A different stone shape and size is needed depending on whether the sculpture is going to be a figure of a person, an angel, or a horse and rider. Some sculptors talk about "freeing" the image that is inside the stone. Sculpting for them is a matter of cutting away the extraneous stone until the fully formed figure emerges. Detail is added over time; with time comes clarity. Your Personal Life Mission is like sculpting a figure in a piece of stone.

Your first PLM statement will not have the detail you wish it would have, but it will gain more definition and detail over the course of the rest of your life. It will take time as you continue to look at your life through what you have learned through this PLM process. But you will choose the stone now.

The size and shape of the stone depend upon what the sculpture is going to be. The same is true of your first PLM statement. I am saying the same general things about my PLM that I was saying ten years ago. My general themes have not changed. But now my PLM has much more clarity and detail to it. Your general themes will not change. You will still have the same core motivations and passions in ten years, but you will understand them much more clearly.

In a year or so, your PLM statement will gain more detail, like a sculptor shaping the facial features of her subject. In a few more years, your PLM statement will have even more detail and clarity, like a sculptor giving texture with fine tools to the hair of her subject.

This is great news! It means that your life can get better. Every year you can better spend your time and energies to do what you are divinely intended to do. It does not mean your life will necessarily get easier, but it will get better and more fulfilling.

Let's begin looking at the options of stone sizes and shapes, and choose one that will fit your sculpture. Let's begin defining our first Personal Life Mission statement.

Define Your Core Competency: What Do You Do Best?

Look at your PLM Worksheet. Look at each of the nine squares, and one by one try to write an action word or a "do" word that expresses something you do well because of what is true about you in that box. For example, my Personality Temperament combination is "Visionary." So a word or statement for that box could be, "I see direction." I could have focused on one of the details of my Personality Temperament or on my summary combination. Here are some examples of what others have put into the boxes: "I communicate truth; I control my life; I break the rules; I grow through

173

adversity." Now you do the same for each box and write them in the boxes below that correspond with the PLM Worksheet boxes.

You may have as many as nine action words or statements or words describing the things you do well if you were able to come up with one for each box. From these nine things you do well, can you boil it down to a statement of what you do best? Write it here:

_____

_____

_____

Another method of defining what you do best is to take a big picture look back at the jobs you have held. Think through your past jobs or major projects you have worked on. What is the best thing you did for the organization or people you worked for? What mark did you leave? How was the place made better or different by what you did? Is there a common theme through your major jobs or projects? If so, write it here:

_____

_____

_____

Another method of defining what you do best is to get feedback. If you have access to a PLM coach, a life coach, or a trusted friend, ask him or her to look at your PLM worksheet and give you observations. Find someone who has been around you plenty in your work. Ask them to tell you what they think you do best. You will probably get several different answers from several people, but some things you did not think of will also probably pleasantly surprise you. Add that to your mix and boil it down to your best stuff.

"I ask good questions," is what Peter Drucker says.

"I mobilize resources," is what Bob Buford (1997) said. Bob Buford built a cable television business in Texas. At midlife, he looked for a way to apply his best stuff to his deepest passion, which was to make an impact for God. We began looking for ways to mobilize the resources of lay people into the action of doing ministry through churches. He started Leadership Network. Leadership Network is a non-profit organization that researches the best methods successful churches are using to mobilize people into ministry. They communicate those discoveries to the rest of the churches who need them.

The result has been a greater stimulation of lay people in churches plugging into ministries.

"I manage my household like a business," was Kathy Peel's (1997) answer. Kathy put her household management methods into print and has sold thousands of copies of her books, *A Mother's Manual for Summer Survival* and *The Family Manager*.

"I line people, organizations, and things up for future success," is my summary of my core ability. This has been my main contribution to the organizations I have worked for, the churches I have pastored, and the individuals I have worked with. I love doing it and much of it comes to me naturally.

It is time to make your final statement of your core competence. Write it down in the My Summary Bridge in Appendix B.

Define Your Target

The next step is defining your target. For, to, with, or on whom will you do your core competence?

Your target may be direct. If you are a physician, your target may be a patient who needs your care. Your target may be indirect. If you are an artist, you are working directly on your art, but there are people who are affected by your art. Who are they?

Do the same kind of exercise with your nine PLM squares for your target that you did for your core competence. Look at your PLM Worksheet and try to think of a target of people who come to your mind as the ones you want to help or impact as you consider your design in each square.

There are a variety of kinds of targets. You target may be defined by:

Gender

Age group

Culture

Need

Location

Interest

I met with a man the other day whose target is Hispanics who have not had a chance to get higher education. He is the director of a university that targets those who typically do not get to go to college. His target is defined by culture and need.

My friend Mark Liederbach wants to impact students on a university campus.

Dr. Bob Pierce, founder of World Vision, began with a desire to help Korean orphans from the Korean War.

With whom have you experienced the greatest success or fulfillment? Who are the people that have benefited the most from what you do? As I look back over my working life, the people whom I have helped the most have been those who were facing life-decisions and wanted direction. They were trying to decide about marriage or college or career or ministry or hiring someone. And they were looking for help in seeing the way. People I have done the least for have been those who did not want or care for direction.

Frequently, I will have parents ask me if I would speak to their adult children, usually of college age, who have no direction in their lives. Most of the time, the problem is that they don't want direction. When I talk to them, it is a waste of my time and theirs. Had their children been interested, they would have come to me themselves. That helps me underscore in my mind who my target is and isn't.

So my target is defined primarily by interest. My target includes males and females. I hit all age groups, but especially those age groups that have a higher percentage of those looking for direction. My target is truly global because a desire for direction is found in cultures all round the world. My location limitations are only defined by my ability to spread PLM information and resources.

Your target may be very broad like mine, or it may be very tight like Dr. Pierce's. Who is your target?

Write the description of your target on your my Summary Bridge in Appendix B. For, to, with, on whom do you do your best work?

You now have the pieces for your first PLM statement. You are choosing the marble stone for your life mission sculpture.

Write Your PLM Summary Statement in One Sentence

"I provide affordable housing to those who need it," says Jack.

"I feed the poorest of the poor," says another.

"I go to the disaster areas of the world and give relief in the name of Jesus Christ," says Franklin Graham.

"I provide auto mechanic help to those who can't afford it," says John.

"I inspire people with confidence that they can do what they have been designed to do," says Tim.

"I write music that moves people to worship God," says Mark.

"I develop properties that serve our community and that support ministries," says Bob.

"I train people to be effective communicators," says Susan.

"I give support and direction to teenagers from broken homes," says Fred.

"I provide financing for upstart ministries," says Bill.

"I provide shelter and help for battered women," says Shirley.

"I give organizational support to a non-profit group that helps people recover from sexual addiction," says Tammy.

"I counsel women from abusive backgrounds," says Karen.

"I am mobilizing 10,000 church planters in third world countries", says Roscoe.

"I teach preschoolers that God loves them," says Betty.

"I help Asian pastors get the resources they need to succeed," says Michael.

"I set up the operational systems for organizations that give educational, counseling, and human development services," says Roy.

"I help street people find a restroom, a shower, a laundry, a meal, God, and a new life," says Everett.

Your PLM Summary Statement is one sentence that says what you do for whom. It is the combination of parts #1 and #2 from your My Summary Bridge in Appendix B.

Now, on your My PLM Statement in Appendix C, write your PLM summary statement in the top three lines.

Congratulations! You have just selected the stone for your life mission sculpture. In ten years your PLM will be clearer, you will see the facial features and details of your sculpture, but we bet it will be essentially the same thing you are saying now.

Your Four "How Tos"

The next part of your PLM statement is four ways you will seek to fulfill your PLM. You may have six ways or two ways. Modify it to fit yourself. Three may be the perfect number. Many feel that three major things are all we can really handle at the same time. The Marines teach the priority of three. Everyone has three major things to focus on and three people on whom to focus.

In this section write the major ways in which you will try to fulfill your PLM.

Here is mine:

My Personal Life Mission is to give life-direction to those who want it. I will seek to fulfill my PLM in these ways:

1. In my family, I will seek to help my wife and children fully discover and fulfill their life purposes.

2. As a pastor, I will help my staff, congregation, and the people of my community discover and fulfill their life purposes.

3. As a writer, speaker, and publisher, I will help people discover and fulfill their life purposes.

What are your major roles in life? I am a husband, father, friend, pastor, community member, writer, speaker, and publisher. As I thought through my key life-roles, it helped me see some key ways I can fulfill my PLM.

What are your best abilities? Your abilities are going to come back in your key ways of fulfilling your PLM. Communication in writing and speaking is one of my abilities from my Abilities box. This is showing up here again in my PLM statement. I am a strategist and visionary in my Personality Temperament box. So in my pastoring I will lead my church strategically to help many people fulfill their PLMs through the structures of our church. I am an entrepreneur and developer in my People Power and

Project Zones, and that will be expressed in my pastoring and publishing works to get the PLM message out to the world.

As you write your key ways of fulfilling your PLM, you need to combine the ideas of your key roles with your key abilities. You may discover you are spending way too much time and energy on something that is not part of your PLM.

That brings us to the third criteria for writing the key ways you will seek to fulfill your PLM. Not only do you consider your roles (or desired roles) and your abilities, but you also have to decide what is the best use of your time and energies. This will be the best time management tool you have ever used.

Now, write in the key ways you are going to fulfill your PLM on your PLM statement.

Your Dreams, Goals, and BHAG's

If you are like me, and I know I am, you are energized by hope. Hope is the idea of good things to come. We can increase our hope by defining the dreams we are living for.

The final section of your PLM statement has fifteen lines. You may want more. This is your section to write out your dreams. What are you living for? Here is the place to say it.

Think about your dreams in these categories:

Spiritually

Family

Friendships

182

Career

Ministry

Financially

Hobbies

These will stimulate your dreams. Brainstorm on another piece of paper about your dreams. Not all dreams have to be earth shattering, but dare to have a few big goals. What would inspire you?

Write at least one BHAG, a Big Hairy Awesome Goal. This is a goal that you are almost afraid to share with others. It inspires you and frightens you at the same time. But if God would allow you to realize it, you could die a very happy camper.

Here are my fifteen as they stand today with a few notes:

1. To grow spiritually throughout my life.

It is part of my belief system that true accomplishment comes from personal depth, which comes from spiritual development. I want a life that never stagnates spiritually.

2. To grow in love with my wife, Greg.

I want my wife to have a romantic and supportive husband who makes her life great. And I want that husband to be me!

3. To prepare my children to fulfill their PLMs.

To give my children the love, discipline, support, and experiences to help them be all God has intended.

4. To earn a good salary and manage it well.

5. To be a life-long learner.

I want a lifestyle of informal and formal learning that deepens me as a person and increases my value to others.

6. To be physically fit throughout my life.

7. To lead my church so that 1,000 people in it are fulfilling their PLMs in various endeavors in our community, so that our church is the number one organization that makes our community better for everyone.

8. To see the PLM process help thousands of people in ministry.

9. To have a home that supports my wife's and my PLMs.

My wife has a creative thing going in her PLM and I have a writing/publishing thing going in mine. We are remodeling our house to create the kinds of workspaces that support both of us and create a great environment for raising our children and entertaining the people God has called us to impact.

10. To write some significant books on leadership and life-direction and a couple of good novels that weave my PLM themes into some great stories.

11. To consult strategic leaders on leadership and life-direction issues.

12. To complete my Ph.D. in Organizational Leadership.

14. To have a place in Mexico and a blue-water fishing boat where I can retreat to fish and write.

I love to saltwater fish in Mexico, and have always loved boats. I want to do the Hemingway thing: write in the mornings, fish in the afternoons.

15. 1 Million PLMs.

This is my BHAG. My Big Hairy Awesome Goal is that through writing, publishing, and speaking, one million people worldwide would discover and pursue their PLMs in my lifetime. It may sound crazy, but I think it can be done.

Now, write the final part of your PLM statement. From your thoughts and notes fill in the fifteen lines, or more, with your dreams, goals, and at least one BHAG.

Congratulations! You have finished your PLM!

Wow, what a journey! You have looked at so many details and tried to summarize where your life is headed. You have chosen the block of stone for your PLM and have begun chiseling away at your sculpture.

You now have in your hands the best life-management tool you could have. With this you can intentionally pursue the design and purpose of your life. Your life can get better and better as you fulfill your purpose more and more.

Now you know what you want to do.

But there is a formula for succeeding at what you want to do that you must understand and apply. How do you get there? How do you fulfill your PLM now that you know what it is? In the next and final chapter we will give you the formula to follow for success. You can reach your dreams if you will do the right things.

Chapter 12

The Formula for Success:
How to Live Your Dreams

"Far better it is to dare mighty things, to win glorious triumphs even though checkered by failure, than to rank with those poor spirits who neither enjoy nor suffer much because they live in the gray twilight that knows neither victory nor defeat."
Theodore Roosevelt

"Opportunity is missed by most people because it is dressed in overalls and looks like work."
Thomas Edison

"The probability that the first job choice you make is right for you is roughly one in a million. If you decide your first choice is the right one, chances are you are just plain lazy."
Peter Drucker

"Awakened to our deepest gifts and aspirations, we know that consideration of calling always has to precede considerations of career and that we can seek the deepest aspirations in work only within the perspectives of calling."
Os Guinness, *The Call*

Living the Dream

Sally, my childhood friend, is running an orphanage in Costa Rica, which she founded. Her goal is to not only make better lives for at-risk children but to raise leaders for the next generation in that country. Her passion and dream began when we were teenagers with a love for Latin American people and cultures.

Mark, my graduate school classmate, is teaching ethics at a university in Virginia. He came from a dysfunctional, alcoholic family in West Virginia. He came from a background that devalued education, but he had a dream to get his education. It grew into a dream to be a university professor where he could have an impact on the minds of college students. After graduate school Mark earned his Ph.D. at the University of

Virginia. Mark came a long way from childhood circumstances because he followed his passion and pursued his dream.

Jack, my friend and parishioner, has come a long way too. Jack, his brother, sister, and mother were abandoned by his father when they were children. In time a stepfather came into their lives but his alcoholism caused the children and their mother tremendous grief. But Jack had a dream to be an influential attorney and politician. He pursued that dream and fought the obstacles in his way. He worked through his Attention Deficit Disorder and found ways to study in school. He attended the University of New Mexico for his undergraduate work. Money was tight so he would go across the street from UNM to a landmark restaurant in Albuquerque, the Frontier. He would spy out people who left food on their plates and he would sit at their tables after they left and finish it for them. Today Jack laughs about it when we travel to Albuquerque and eat at the Frontier. He can laugh now. Jack is the most influential attorney in our city and he fills an elected position in our county and a governor-appointed position in our state government. He had a passion and he followed a dream.

Finding your passion and living your dream does not come automatically. Success does not bite us on the behind and say, "Here I am". It also does not come through a bunch of loud hype. Success comes through a process that can be expressed in a formula. For some reason some people struggle more to "get" this formula than others. Some people's lives seem to follow the formula easier than others. Regardless of whether this comes to you easily or not, you have to get this. Get this life-changing concept down so you can follow it and live the life you were meant to.

Sally, Mark, and Jack all got this concept and they are living their dreams. You can too.

The Formula for Success

Here is the formula for living your dreams, and succeeding:

Value & Com. + Capability + Work – Idiot = Success.

This formula should be read like this:

Your Value and Commitment to a Purpose

Plus Your Capability to Fulfill that Purpose

Plus The Work You Do Toward the Purpose

Minus Your Idiot

Equals Your Success.

This formula is true and it is gold if you will apply it. I pastor a large congregation and I have dealt with hundreds of my parishioners over the years on these very practical matters of finding a direction for life and work. The ones who succeed follow this formula, the ones who don't, don't succeed. It even applies to those who would aspire to work in the field of religion. Success doesn't just come because you have a worthy purpose, the whole formula applies. The Bible is incredibly practical. This formula is supported by the wisdom of the great biblical book of Proverbs. One example is the Proverb that says, "The sluggard craves and gets nothing, but the desires of the diligent are fully satisfied" (Proverbs 13:4 NIV). Desire is not enough; it must be followed with diligence in the right direction.

My educational track has taken me through the humanities and particularly to the social sciences of leadership and organizational development. Organizational leadership authorities agree with our formula as it applies to the success of potential leaders (Bass, 1990, Jacques, 1998). Wanting to be a leader is good but there has to be leadership capability, proper work toward leadership effectiveness, and an absence of idiotic behaviors that sabotage leadership for a potential leader to succeed.

I have been a personal career consultant as an associate with Steve Johnson for ten years. My association with Steve began years ago when I was personally floundering and looking for my purpose. Steve's wise counsel helped me find focus on my passion and dreams. Steve's process brought me to the place where I could grasp this formula. I have used it as a staple of my consulting and training with those who want to get their careers on track and I have seen it produce success.

This isn't rocket science. Most great things aren't. But this is gold for your success.

This formula has five major parts to it: four factors and one result.

Value & Com. + Capability + Work − Idiot = Success.

Value and Commitment

Value means it is important to you. Commitment means you will work hard at it even when you face set backs, obstacles, problems, and failures. Value & Commitment are first in the formula for a reason; it is the most important factor. It is also the initial factor that gets everything else rolling in the right direction. Everything begins with you *wanting to do something*. Another way of saying this is "motivation." You have to be motivated or you won't get anywhere.

This is why we spent eleven chapters and you have spent a lot of work on defining your Personal Life Mission. Your PLM is the first part of this formula. Your PLM is what you value and will commit to. Your deep desire is the fuel that is going to drive the whole process of reaching your dreams.

For review write your Personal Life Mission Statement again here:

_____

_____

_____

Okay, this is the first factor of your success. Let's look at the second.

Capabilities

By "capabilities" we mean the things you can now do that are in line with your dream. We are not trying to uncover every possible thing you can do. I can pop my belly button out so it is an "outie" but that capability has never advanced me toward my passion and dreams. So we don't care about your irrelevant capabilities. We are trying to uncover what you can do that will help you get where you want to be. This process is important because it will not only reveal what you have, but what you don't have yet. Yet is the key word here. The capabilities you don't have yet but will need to reach your dreams are your *punch-list for preparation*. There is some knowledge you probably don't have yet but will be able to pick up through informal learning or formal education. There are some skills you don't have yet but will be able to acquire through practice. There are some abilities you don't have yet, but they can probably be acquired through persistence.

Passion and dreams are important but they are only the beginning. Capabilities have to be added to our passion and dreams. You may want to be a doctor very badly, but until you add the knowledge, skills, and abilities of a doctor you might as well wish in one hand and spit in the other and see which one fills up first.

List here the knowledge you now have that can help you reach your PLM:

_____

_____

_____

List here the skills you now have that can help you reach your PLM:

_____

_____

_____

List here the abilities you now have that can help you reach your PLM.

_____

_____

_____

Work

Work is solving problems. This is true of mental or physical work. When your laundry piles up, you have to solve the problem of doing the wash. When we have the problem of needing fuel for our cars, someone has to do the work of drilling for oil, refining it, and shipping it to our gas station. Many problems are solved in that process: it takes all kinds of work.

Work is the third factor in the equation of success. Not only must you Value & Commit to something and have some Capability for it but you must also do the Work to solve the problems on the road toward your dream.

There are three kinds of work or problem solving you must do. First, you must do the work of preparing yourself to achieve your passion and dream. When you discover what capabilities you don't yet have but need to accomplish your dream, you have your work-order for your preparation. "Luck is when preparation meets opportunity," is a common proverb, and we believe it. The unprepared are passed over by opportunity like wilted lettuce in the produce section.

List here what knowledge, skills, and abilities you need to acquire to fulfill your PLM:

_____

_____

_____

Adding to your capabilities is probably going to require some kind of formal or informal education. Alvin Toffler has said, "The illiterate of the future will not be the person who cannot read. It will be the person who does not know how to learn."

Being a person who lives their dream means being a person who lives a life of learning. According to *USA Today* (1997) in 1979 a full-time male worker over age 25 with a four-year college degree earned 49% more a year on average than a worker with only a high-school diploma. That gap widened to 89% by 1995 according to the 1996 *Economic Report of the President*. Also, each year of formal schooling after high school adds 5% to 15% to annual earnings later in life, the report says.

You may not need formal education. You may be able to pick up new capabilities by reading on your own and practicing new skills. That's how the author Jack London did it. But if you do need formal education, do what it takes to fulfill your purpose.

Second, you must do the work of solving the opportunity problem. The opportunity problem is getting the chance to do what you want to do. There are two sides to the opportunity problem. The first is blooming in the opportunity where you are now. The second is reaching out and seizing the next level of opportunity toward your goal. Few people go from being a bum to be being a corporate CEO. Most successes come in upward steps. Many people stagnate at one level for a long time because they have no dream to go anywhere higher. Some dream of rising to higher achievement, but they will not pay the price of working through the steps that lead up to it.

List some steps you should take to do better where you are or to reach higher by attempting new things:

_____

_____

_____

You might rise higher in your job by doing better now. You might need to apply for a higher position. You might need to change departments. You might need to work for someone else or for yourself.

Third, you must do the work of recovering from failure with new hope and smarter methods. Most people are not taught to fail well. We believe you will fail if you are normal. We have failed; and frankly, we don't care much for people who haven't tasted it along their way to success. The difference between those who stick to their passion and reach their dream and those who don't is their willingness to do the work of recovering from failure. Failure is a problem. But it is mostly a problem between our ears.

List the things you have learned from your last greatest failure that will help you worker smarter toward your goals now:

_____

_____

_____

Peter Drucker says, "Everything boils down to work." He's right and we would be liars to try to tell you that you can find your passion and live your dream without work. But when you work in the direction of your dream, it is work that is worth the sacrifice and effort.

Managing Your Idiot

In the movie *Dirty Rotten Scoundrels* Michael Cane and Steve Martin play two hustlers in the south of France who try to con wealthy women out of their money. Cane's character promises to teach Martin's character his tricks of the trade if he will play along as an idiot little brother named Ruprect. Cane romances wealthy women but they realize they can't marry him when they meet Ruprect. Ruprect does all kinds of crazy and bizarre things that scare the women and sabotage any possible marriage, which was part of their plan anyway.

You have a Ruprect that lives inside you. That is not a personal insult. It is the truth about the human condition. You have an idiot who will try to sabotage your success. That is why the formula for success reads "- Idiot." We need to lessen the impact of our idiot. The more he or she shows up, the less we succeed--the more he or she is controlled, the more we can succeed.

Freud used a shorter word to describe it, "Id" (Miller, 1993). The id was Freud's concept of our innate desires. The id drives us for immediate satisfaction of our most base wants. C.S. Hall called the id the "spoiled child of the personality" (Miller, 1993). Freud described the "Superego" as the mechanism we would call conscience and it makes the id behave. Freud was seeking to explain a human experience we all have. We feel divided within ourselves between proper desires and improper ones.

Some Catholics refer to the better angels within us. In contrast they sometimes say we all have our demons. This is a classic expression of how we struggle between our divided natures.

The Apostle Paul said he was so divided between himself that he did not do the things he wanted to do and he did the things he did not want to do (Romans 7:15). He says the struggle for Christians is between the flesh and the spirit (Galatians 5).

Let's keep it simple. We all have an idiot that we have to suppress or change to keep from ruining the good we are trying to do. I have my idiot. He shows up at some of the most unexpected and unappreciated times. And you have yours.

Some people have let their idiot take over. We all know people like this. It seems we all have some in our families who have promoted their idiot to captain of their ship. The idiot may abuse drugs and alcohol. She may be a control freak or hypercritical. He may be abusive or lazy. This makes holidays very interesting. Unfortunately it causes havoc in the idiot owner's life and others suffer along with them.

Others have let their idiot rise to partner. He is not the controlling partner at all times, but he gets more say than he deserves and the result is a diminished life and hurt for others.

Take our challenge to shut down your idiot. Your passion and dreams will come much easier when they don't have to face him. And when you do succeed, you can succeed successfully.

What is your idiot's profile? What are his or her tendencies? Our idiots tend to be insecure, fearful, and escapist. Think through this profile.

What are your idiot's insecurities? Why does your idiot feel like others do not like him or her or in what way does your idiot feel inferior to others? You have to overcome your idiot's insecurities by affirming your value. God affirms you and it really doesn't matter if anyone else does. So keep your idiot under control on this one.

What are your idiot's fears? What bad things does your idiot keep telling you are going to happen? Our idiots tend to create these awful paranoid fears in our minds that something bad is going to happen and it will be the end of life, as we know it on planet earth. Nonsense! Most things we worry about never happen. We waste a ton of energy on anxiety. Then when bad things do happen, we can survive them much better than we ever thought. In fact, God promises to not allow anything bad into our lives unless he also supplies us the necessary strength to endure and keep fulfilling his purpose in us (I Corinthians 10:14).

How does your idiot try to escape? Our idiots try to derail our effectiveness by leading us to escape from our problems and challenges in unhealthy ways. We can escape with food, sex, drugs, alcohol, spending money, gambling, laziness, work-a-holism, and just about anything done to excess.

Escapism is an attempt to medicate pain we have in our hearts. There are several ways everyone can properly medicate pains of the heart. First, Jesus Christ invites everyone who will to come to him by faith and he will give them spiritual rest and peace. We have spent an entire book helping you discover your personal design. May we propose to you that behind your personal design there really is a Designer? We believe this Designer is the creator of heaven and earth who has communicated to us in several ways. By the creation of earth and the universe he communicates his wisdom, power, and appreciation for beauty and balance. He spoke to spiritual people in the past who wrote his message down in the scriptures, the Bible. His highest point of communication to man was by taking on human nature and personally coming to the earth as Jesus Christ. His on-going way of communicating to us is through His Spirit who speaks to our hearts. His core message is that God wants to be in relationship with us. He created us and designed us for a purpose. And that relationship and purpose can be fully realized when we give our lives in faith to the Lord Jesus Christ.

Second, when we come to Christ by faith he gives us his Holy Spirit and his Spirit helps give us peace in the midst of our life-storms.

Third, we must take seriously our personal growth both spiritually and mentally. If you have come to Christ, your growth in knowing him must be the first priority of your life. From there everything else can flow properly. It is Christ who ultimately calls you to your PLM and it is Christ who will sustain you through all the ups and downs of life on the way to fulfilling your purpose. You can grow spiritually by involvement in a good church, by meeting with friends who are growing in Christ also, and by studying the Bible and the great materials on the Christian life that are readily available today.

Part of your mental development is learning to think right. In addition to the good Christian literature that is available, we also recommend *Feeling Good* by Dr. David Burns and *Life Strategies* by Dr. Phillip McGraw. Both of these authors have captured practical and important ideas about managing our idiots and thinking straight.

Success

Finally, be ready to succeed successfully or don't waste your time. Please, for the sake of mankind, the planet, and God himself, use your success for the benefit of others. Help others succeed, and win at the ultimate character challenge, the challenge of success.

I believe if you follow the wisdom of this book, you will succeed in finding your passion and living your dream.

Success is going to mean so many different things to the people who read this book because God will call people to so many different yet good Personal Life Missions.

Review the Formula for Success

Here is the formula for success one more time. Underneath each part of the formula are some blank lines where you can journal your thoughts. Jot down actions you will take. Under "Success" jot down what success will look like when you are fulfilling your PLM.

Value & Com. + Capability + Work − Idiot = Success

____	____	____	____	____
____	____	____	____	____
____	____	____	____	____
____	____	____	____	____
____	____	____	____	____
____	____	____	____	____
____	____	____	____	____

Join Us as PLM Partners

This has been an important journey for all who have gone through the whole PLM process. Now you are beginning a new journey, pursuing your PLM. We would like to hear from you. There is a place on our website www.TheJohnMorganCompany.com where we invite you to register your Personal Life Mission statement. Remember my BHAG is one million people pursuing their PLMs? If you have written your PLM statement, we would like to hear from you.

World Changers

When God created people, he gave them the purpose of managing his whole earth (Genesis 2:23). Psalms 24:1 says, "The earth is the Lord's and everything in it" (NIV). In Matthew 28:18 Christ expanded our mission to making disciples of all people groups on the earth.

The expansion of the Christian mission in evangelism did not erase the former mission of being God's agents in every part of his world. We are God's people who are called to bring God's blessings of justice, equality, freedom, beauty, and harmony to every part of the world and human society. We are to be his people in every worthy field of human work: in agriculture, medicine, law, business, education, art, government, military, and religion.

As we all fulfill our Personal Life Missions from God, we are doing his part to change lives, to change the world, and to honor our Maker.

May God bless you as you do your part.

"God has called us, and we are never more ourselves than when we are fully stretched in answering" (Os Guinness, *The Call).*

My PLM Worksheet

My Design From My Past	My Present Personality Wiring	Forces Drawing Me to My Destiny
Life Highlights 1. 2. 3.	**Personal Temperament** 1. Internal 67 % 2. Futurist 80 % 3. Thinker 67 % 4. Planner 67 % Combo: Themes:	**Interests** 1. 2. 3. 4. 5.
Life Intersections 1. 2. 3.	**My People Power** 1._____ ___% 2._____ ___% 3._____ ___% 4._____ ___% Combo: Themes:	**Essential Outcomes** 1. 2. 3.
Abilities 1. 2. 3.	**My Project Zone** Conc. Create Dev. Ref. Max. __% __% __% __% __% My Range: My Motivation: My Demotivation:	**Passion** I am moved by: I hate: If God would let me:

My Summary Bridge

The Summary Bridge from

My PLM Worksheet to

My Personal Life Mission

My Core Competency
What I do best

_____

_____

_____

My Target
Whom I want to do this for

_____

_____

_____

Name _____

Date _____

Location _____

My PLM Statement

My Personal Life Mission
(do what for whom?)

_____

_____

_____

Some key ways I will seek to do this:

1. _____
2. _____
3. _____
4. _____

Some of my life goals and dreams:

1. _____
2. _____
3. _____
4. _____
5. _____
6. _____
7. _____
8. _____
9. _____
10. _____

References

Barnhart, R.K. (1988). *The Barnhart Concise Dictionary of Etymology: The Origins of American English words.* NY: Harper Collins.

Bass, B.M. (1990). Bass *& Stogdill's Handbook of Leadership: Theory, Research, & Management Applications*, 3rd edition. New York: The Free Press.

Buford, B., Drucker, P.F. & Whalin, T. (1997). *Half time: Changing your game plan from success to significance.* Grand Rapids, MI: Zondervan.

Burns, D.D. (1980). *Feeling good: The new mood therapy*. New York: Signet.

Drucker, P. (1979). *The effective executive.* New York: Harper & Row.

Drucker, P. (1989). *The new realities in government and politics/in economics and business/in society and world view.* New York: Harper & Row.

Drucker, P. (1991). *Adventures of a bystander: Memoirs.* HarperCollins.

Dyer, D. (1997). *Jack London: A biography.* New York: Scholastic, Inc.

Gardner, H. (1995). *Leading minds: An anatomy of leadership.* New York: HarperCollins.

Guinness, O. (1998). *The call: Finding and fulfilling the central purpose of your life.* Nashville, TN: Word Publishing.

Hatch, M.J. (1997). *Organization theory: Modern symbolic and postmodern perspectives.* New York: Oxford University Press.

The Holy Bible. (1984). *The New International Version.* Grand Rapids, MI: Zondervan.

Jacques, E. & Cason, K. (1994). *Human capability.* Arlington, VA: Cason Hall Publishers.

Jacques, E. (1998). *Requisite organization: A total system for effective managerial Organization and managerial leadership for the 21st century.* Arlington, VA:Cason Hall Publishers.

Jung, C.G. (1971*). Psychological types* (R.F.C. Hall, Trans.). Princeton, NJ: Princeton University Press.

Klopp, H. & Tarcy, B. (1994). *The adventure of leadership: an unorthodox business guide by the man who conquered 'the North Face'.*

McGraw, P.C. (1999). *Life strategies: Doing what works, doing what matters.* New York: Hyperion.

Maslow, A.H. (1954). *Motivation and personality.* New York: Harper.

Miller, P.H. (1993). *Theories of Developmental Psychology.* W.H. Freeman and Company.

Peel, B. & Peel, K. (1997). *Discover your destiny: Finding the courage to follow your dreams.* Colorado Springs, CO: NavPress.

Schultz, W. (1958). *FIRO: A three-dimensional theory of interpersonal behavior.* New York: Holt, Rinehart, & Winston.

Shanahan, M. & Schefter, A. (1999). *Think like a champion: Building success one victory at a time.* New York, Harper Business.

Sheehy, G. (1995). *New passages: Mapping your life across time.* New York: Random House.

Warner, M. (1999). *American sermons: The pilgrims to Martin Luther Kin, Jr.* New York: Literary Classics of America. New York: Berkley.

Also available from Dr. John Morgan

This book is a unique and powerful tool that can help high-capacity leaders double their effectiveness. This book is the best of Dr. Morgan's doctoral studies and research on leadership. It explains in straight forward language what the essential nature of leadership is and it explains why there are different levels of leadership capability among people.

Understanding and working with people who have different levels of leadership capability is a key to building the kind of organization that will fulfill the vision of a high-capacity leader.

This book will teach you:
- 7 Laws of Leadership Horsepower
- 5 Ways to Maximize Your Leadership
- How to Design Your Organization for Maximum Results
- Your Current Leadership Level
- Your Future Leadership Potential
- Whom You Need in Your Organization to Succeed

Available from Amazon.com or XulonPress.com/bookstore.php

To learn more about the Leadership Horsepower SeminarTM or to register your PLM, visit: **www.TheJohnMorganCompany.com**.